Political Philosophy: A Very Short Introduction

VERY SHORT INTRODUCTIONS are for anyone wanting a stimulating and accessible way into a new subject. They are written by experts, and have been translated into more than 45 different languages.

The series began in 1995, and now covers a wide variety of topics in every discipline. The VSI library now contains over 500 volumes—a Very Short Introduction to everything from Psychology and Philosophy of Science to American History and Relativity—and continues to grow in every subject area.

Titles in the series include the following:

David Miller

POLITICAL PHILOSOPHY

A Very Short Introduction

OXFORD
UNIVERSITY PRESS

OXFORD

UNIVERSITY PRESS

Great Clarendon Street, Oxford OX2 6DP

Oxford University Press is a department of the University of Oxford.
It furthers the University's objective of excellence in research, scholarship,
and education by publishing worldwide in

Oxford New York

Auckland Bangkok Buenos Aires Cape Town Chennai
Dar es Salaam Delhi Hong Kong Istanbul Karachi Kolkata
Kuala Lumpur Madrid Melbourne Mexico City Mumbai Nairobi
São Paulo Shanghai Taipei Tokyo Toronto

Oxford is a registered trade mark of Oxford University Press
in the UK and in certain other countries

Published in the United States
by Oxford University Press Inc., New York

© David Miller 2003

The moral rights of the author have been asserted
Database right Oxford University Press (maker)

First published as a Very Short Introduction 2003

British Library Cataloguing in Publication Data

Data available

Library of Congress Cataloging in Publication Data

Data available

ISBN 978-0-19-280395-5

26

Typeset by RefineCatch Ltd, Bungay, Suffolk
Printed and bound by CPI Group (UK) Ltd, Croydon, CR0 4YY

Contents

Preface

I wanted this book to make political philosophy engaging and accessible to people who had never encountered it before, and so I have tried hard to write as simply as possible without sacrificing accuracy. Explaining some fairly abstract ideas without lapsing into the technical jargon that deadens so much academic writing today proved to be an interesting challenge. I am extremely grateful to friends from different walks of life who agreed to read the first draft of the manuscript, and along with general encouragement made many helpful suggestions: Graham Anderson, George Brown, Sue Miller, Elaine Poole, and Adam Swift, as well as two readers from Oxford University Press. I should also like to thank Zofia Stemplowska for invaluable help in preparing the final manuscript.

List of illustrations

Chapter 1
Why do we need political philosophy?

This is a small book about a big subject, and since a picture is
proverbially worth a thousand words I want to begin it by talking
about a very large picture that can help us to see what political
philosophy is all about. The picture in question was painted
between 1337 and 1339 by Ambrogio Lorenzetti, and it covers
three walls of the Sala dei Nove in the Palazzo Pubblico of Siena.
It is usually called the *Allegory of Good and Bad Government*, and
what Lorenzetti's frescos do is first of all to depict the nature of
good and bad government respectively by means of figures who
represent the qualities that rulers ought and ought not to have,
and then to show the effects of the two kinds of government on
the lives of ordinary people. So in the case of good government we
see the dignified ruler dressed in rich robes and sitting on his
throne, surrounded by figures representing the virtues of Courage,
Justice, Magnanimity, Peace, Prudence, and Temperance. Beneath
him stand a line of citizens encircled by a long rope the ends of
which are tied to the ruler's wrist, symbolizing the harmonious
binding together of ruler and people. As we turn to the right we
see Lorenzetti's portrayal of the effects of good government first in
the city and then in the countryside. The city is ordered and
wealthy: we see artisans plying their trades, merchants buying and
selling goods, nobles riding gaily decorated horses; in one place a
group of dancers join hands in a circle. Beyond the city gate a
well-dressed lady rides out to hunt, passing on the way a plump

saddleback pig being driven in to market; in the countryside itself peasants till the earth and gather in the harvest. In case any careless viewer should fail to grasp the fresco's message, it is spelt out in a banner held aloft by a winged figure representing Security:

> Without fear every man may travel freely and each may till and sow, so long as this commune still maintains this lady sovereign, for she has stripped the wicked of all power.

The fresco on the other side, representing evil government, is less well preserved, but its message is equally plain: a demonic ruler surrounded by vices like Avarice, Cruelty, and Pride, a city under military occupation, and a barren countryside devastated by ghostly armies. Here the inscription held by the figure of Fear reads:

> Because each seeks only his own good, in this city Justice is subjected to tyranny; wherefore along this road nobody passes without fearing for his life, since there are robberies outside and inside the city gates.

There is no better way to understand what political philosophy is and why we need it than by looking at Lorenzetti's magnificent mural. We can define political philosophy as an investigation into the nature, causes, and effects of good and bad government, and our picture not only encapsulates this quest, but expresses in striking visual form three ideas that stand at the very heart of the subject. The first is that good and bad government profoundly affect the quality of human lives. Lorenzetti shows us how the rule of justice and the other virtues allows ordinary people to work, trade, hunt, dance, and generally do all those things that enrich human existence, while on the other side of the picture, tyranny breeds poverty and death. So that is the first idea: it really makes a difference to our lives whether we are governed well or badly. We cannot turn our back on politics, retreat into private life, and imagine that the way we are governed will not have profound effects on our personal happiness.

The second idea is that the form our government takes is not predetermined: we have a choice to make. Why, after all, was the mural painted in the first place? It was painted in the Sala dei Nove – the Room of the Nine – and these Nine were the rotating council of nine wealthy merchants who ruled the city in the first half of the 14th century. So it served not only to remind these men of their responsibilities to the people of Siena, but also as a celebration of the republican form of government that had been established there, at a time of considerable political turmoil in many of the Italian cities. The portrayal of evil government was not just an academic exercise: it was a reminder of what might happen if the rulers of the city failed in their duty to the people, or if the people failed in *their* duty to keep a watchful eye on their representatives.

The third idea is that we can know what distinguishes good government from bad: we can trace the effects of different forms of government, and we can learn what qualities go to make up the best form of government. In other words, there is such a thing as political knowledge. Lorenzetti's frescos bear all the marks of this idea. As we have seen, the virtuous ruler is shown surrounded by figures representing the qualities that, according to the political philosophy of the age, characterized good government. The frescos are meant to be instructive: they are meant to teach both rulers and citizens how to achieve the kind of life that they wanted. And this presupposes, as Lorenzetti surely believed, that we can know how this is to be done.

Should we believe the message of the frescos, however? Are the claims they implicitly make actually *true*? Does it really make a difference to our lives what kind of government we have? Do we have any choice in the matter, or is the form of our government something over which we have no control? And can we know what

1. The virtuous ruler from *The Allegory of Good and Bad Government* by Ambrogio Lorenzetti.

makes one form of government better than another? These are some of the big questions that political philosophers ask, as well as many smaller ones. But before trying to answer them, I need to add a few more words of explanation.

When talking about government here, I mean something much broader than 'the government of the day' – the group of people in authority in any society at a particular moment. Indeed I mean something broader than the state – the political institutions through which authority is exercised, such as the cabinet of ministers, parliament, courts of law, police, armed forces, and so forth. I mean the whole body of rules, practices and institutions under whose guidance we live together in societies. That human beings need to cooperate with one another, to know who can do what with whom, who owns which parts of the material world, what happens if somebody breaks the rules, and so forth, we can

4

perhaps take for granted here. But we cannot yet take it for granted that they must have a state to solve these problems. As we shall see in the next chapter, one central issue in political philosophy is why we need states, or more generally political authority, in the first place, and we need to engage with the anarchist argument that societies can perfectly well govern themselves without it. So for the time being, I want to leave it an open question whether 'good government' requires having a state, or a government in the conventional sense, at all. Another question that will remain open until the last chapter of the book is whether there should be just one government or many governments – a single system for the whole of humanity, or different systems for different peoples.

When Lorenzetti painted his murals, he presented good and bad government primarily in terms of the human qualities of the two kinds of rulers, and the effects those qualities had on the lives of their subjects. Given the medium in which the message was conveyed, this was perhaps unavoidable, but in any case it was very much in line with the thinking of his age. Good government was as much about the character of those who governed – their prudence, courage, generosity, and so on – as about the system of government itself. Of course there were also debates about the system: about whether monarchy was preferable to republican government or vice versa, for instance. Today the emphasis has changed: we think much more about the institutions of good government, and less about the personal qualities of the people who make them work. Arguably we have gone too far in this direction, but I will follow modern fashion and talk in later chapters primarily about good government as a system, not about how to make our rulers virtuous.

Back now to the ideas behind the big picture. The easiest of the three to defend is the idea that government profoundly affects the quality of our lives. If any reader fails to recognize this straight away, it is perhaps because he or she is living under a relatively

5

stable form of government where not much changes from year to year. One party replaces another at election time, but the switch only makes a marginal impact on most people's lives (though politicians like to pretend otherwise). But think instead about some of the regimes that rose and fell in the last century: think about the Nazi regime in Germany and the 6 million Jews who were killed by it, or think about Mao's China and the 20 million or more who died as a result of the famine induced by the so-called 'Great Leap Forward'. Meanwhile in other countries whole populations saw their living standards rise at an unprecedented rate. Twentieth-century history seems to have reproduced the stark contrast of Lorenzetti's mural almost exactly.

But at this point we have to consider the second of our three ideas. Even if different forms of government were, and still are, direct causes of prosperity and poverty, life and death, how far are we able to influence the regimes that govern us? Or are they just links in a chain, themselves governed by deeper causes over which we have no control? And if so, what is the point of political philosophy, whose avowed purpose is to help us choose the best form of government?

The fatalistic view that we have no real political choices to make has appeared in different forms at different times in history. In the period when Lorenzetti was painting his frescos, many believed that history moved in cycles: good government could not endure, but would inevitably become corrupted with the passage of time, collapse into tyranny, and only through slow stages be brought back to its best form. In other periods – most notably the 19th century – the prevailing belief was in the idea of historical progress: history moved in a straight line from primitive barbarism to the higher stages of civilization. But once again this implied that the way societies were governed depended on social causes that were not amenable to human control. The most influential version of this was Marxism, which held that the development of society depended ultimately on the way in which people produced material goods –

the technology they used, and the economic system they adopted. Politics became part of the 'superstructure'; it was geared to the needs of the prevailing form of production. So, according to Marx, in capitalist societies the state had to serve the interests of the capitalist class, in socialist societies it would serve the interests of the workers, and eventually, under communism, it would disappear completely. In this light, speculation about the best form of government becomes pointless: history will solve the problem for us.

Interestingly enough, the career of Marxism itself shows us what is wrong with this kind of determinism. Under the influence of Marxist ideas, socialist revolutions broke out in places where, according to Marx, they should not have occurred – in societies such as Russia and China which were relatively undeveloped economically, and therefore not ready to adopt a socialist form of production. In the more advanced capitalist societies, meanwhile, fairly stable democratic governments were established in some places – something Marx had thought impossible given the class divided nature of these societies – while other countries fell prey to fascist regimes. Politics, it turned out, was to a considerable extent independent of economics, or of social development more generally. And this meant that once again people had big choices to make, not only about their form of government in the narrow sense, but about the broader way their society was constituted. Should they have a one-party state or a liberal democracy with free elections? Should the economy be centrally planned or based on the free market? These are questions of the sort that political philosophers try to answer, and they were once more back on the agenda.

But if 20th-century experience put paid to the kind of historical determinism that was so prevalent in the 19th, by the beginning of the 21st a new form of fatalism had appeared. This was inspired by the growth of a new global economy, and the belief that states had increasingly little room for manœuvre if they wanted their people to benefit from it. Any state that tried to buck the market would find that its economy slumped. And the only states that were likely to succeed in the new global competition were the liberal democracies, so although it was possible for a society to be governed differently – to have an Islamic regime, for example – the price for this would be relative economic decline: a price, it was assumed, no society would wish to pay. This was the so-called 'end of history' thesis, essentially a claim that all societies would be propelled by economic forces into governing themselves in roughly the same way.

There is little doubt that this form of fatalism will be undermined by events just as earlier forms were. Already we can see a backlash against globalization in the form of political movements concerned about the environment, or the impact of global markets on developing nations, or the levelling-down quality of global culture. These movements challenge the idea that economic growth is the supreme goal, and in the course of doing so raise questions about what we ultimately value in our lives, and how we can achieve these aims, that are central questions of political philosophy. And even if we confine ourselves to political debate that lies closer to the conventional centre ground, there is still plenty of scope to argue about how much economic freedom we should sacrifice in the name of greater equality, or how far personal liberty should be restricted in order to strengthen the communities in which we live. As I write, there is a fierce argument going on about terrorism, the rights of individuals, and the principle that we cannot interfere in the internal affairs of other states, no matter how they are governed. Once again these are issues over which collective choices have to be made, and they are quintessentially issues of political philosophy.

So far I have argued that political philosophy deals with issues that are of vital importance to all of us, and furthermore issues over which we have real political choices to make. Now I want to confront another reason for dismissing the whole subject, namely that politics is about the use of power, and powerful people – politicians especially – do not pay any attention to works of political philosophy. If you want to change things, according to this line of thought, you should go out on the streets, demonstrate, and cause some chaos, or alternatively perhaps see if you can find a politician to bribe or blackmail, but you shouldn't bother with learned treatises on the good society that nobody reads.

It is true that when political philosophers have tried to intervene directly in political life, they have usually come unstuck. They have advised powerful rulers – Aristotle acted as tutor to Alexander the Great, Machiavelli attempted to counsel the Medicis in Florence, and Diderot was invited to St Petersburg by Catherine the Great to discuss how to modernize Russia – but whether these interventions did any good is another question. Treatises written during times of intense political conflict have often succeeded merely in alienating both sides to the conflict. A famous example is Thomas Hobbes's *Leviathan*, a masterpiece of political philosophy written while the English Civil War was still raging. Hobbes's arguments in favour of absolute government, which I shall discuss more fully in the following chapter, were welcomed neither by the Royalists nor by the Parliamentarians. The former believed that kings had been divinely ordained to rule, the latter that legitimate government required the consent of its subjects. The bleak picture of the human condition painted by Hobbes led him to the conclusion that we must submit to any established and effective government, no matter what its credentials were. By implication Charles I had a right to rule when he was in power, but so did Cromwell when he had succeeded in deposing Charles. This was not what either side wanted to hear.

The example of Hobbes can help to explain why political philosophers have so rarely made a *direct* impact on political events. Because they look at politics from a philosophical perspective, they are bound to challenge many of the conventional beliefs held both by politicians and by the public at large. They put these beliefs under the microscope, asking exactly what people mean when they say such and such, what evidence they have for their convictions, how they would justify their beliefs if challenged to do so. One result of this forensic examination is that when political philosophers put forward their own ideas and proposals, these nearly always look strange and disturbing to those who are used to the conventional debate, as Hobbes's ideas did to those fighting on both sides in the Civil War.

But this does not stop political philosophy from having an influence, sometimes a considerable influence, with the passage of time. When we think about politics, we make assumptions that we are often barely aware of – underlying assumptions that nevertheless do change quite radically over the course of history. At the time Hobbes wrote, for instance, it was commonplace to argue politically by appeal to religious principles, and especially to the authority of the Bible. One of his lasting legacies was to make it possible to think about politics in a purely secular way. Although Hobbes himself was deeply preoccupied with religious questions, his radically new approach to political authority allowed politics and religion to be separated and discussed in different terms. Or consider that in Hobbes's time, only a few extreme radicals believed in democracy as a form of government (typically, Hobbes himself did not rule it out altogether, but he thought it was generally inferior to monarchy). Nowadays, of course, we take democracy for granted to the extent that we can barely imagine how any other form of government could be seen as legitimate. How has this change come about? The story is a complex one, but an indispensable part in it has been played by political philosophers arguing in favour of democracy, philosophers whose ideas were taken up, popularized, and cast into the mainstream of politics. The best known of these is probably Jean-Jacques Rousseau, whose impact on the French Revolution through his book *The Social Contract* is hard to dispute. (Thomas Carlyle, at least, had no doubts. Challenged to show the practical importance of abstract ideas, he is said to have replied, 'There was once a man called Rousseau who wrote a book containing nothing but ideas. The second edition was bound in the skins of those who had laughed at the first.')

Nobody can tell in advance whether any given work of political thought will have the effect of Hobbes's *Leviathan* or Rousseau's *Social Contract*, or to take a later example, Marx and Engels's *The Communist Manifesto*. It depends entirely on whether the underlying shift in thinking that the philosopher proposes corresponds to political and social change in such a way that the new ideas can become the commonplaces of the following generations. Other works of political philosophy have enjoyed a limited success and then disappeared virtually without trace. But the need for political philosophy is always there, especially perhaps at moments when we face new political challenges that we cannot deal with using the conventional wisdom of the day. At these moments we need to dig deeper, to probe the basis of our political beliefs, and it is here that we may turn to political philosophy, not perhaps at source, but as filtered through pamphlets, magazines, newspapers and the like – every successful political philosopher has relied on media-friendly disciples to put his or her ideas into circulation.

But even if political philosophy answers to a genuine need, are its own credentials genuine? (Horoscopes answer to a strongly felt need – people want to know what the future holds in store for them – but most of us think that horoscopes themselves are completely bogus.) For political philosophy claims that it can bring to us a kind of *truth* about politics, something different from the *opinions* that guide us from day to day. This claim was presented most dramatically by Plato, often regarded as the father of the subject, through the allegory of the cave in the *Republic*. Plato likens ordinary people to prisoners who have been chained in a cave in such a way that they can only see the shadows of things on a screen in front of them; they would

ac ke te tables. con a bone, otheother be nethe.]An cut boñ are ertra ben

2. Plato and Socrates, frontispiece by Matthew Paris (*d.* 1259) for *The Prognostics of Socrates the King.*

assume, Plato says, that these shadows were the only real things. Now suppose that one of the prisoners was to be freed and emerged blinking into the light. In time he would come to see real objects in the world, and understand that what he had seen before *were* no more than shadows. But if he were then to return to the cave to try to persuade his fellows of their mistake, they would be unlikely to believe him. This, Plato thinks, is the position of the philosopher: he has genuine knowledge while those around him have only distorted opinions, but because the path to philosophical knowledge is long and hard, very few are willing to take it.

But was Plato justified in drawing such a sharp contrast between philosophical knowledge and common opinion? This is not the place to discuss the metaphysical underpinning of his distinction, so let me say simply that my conception of political philosophy does not involve endowing philosophers with a special kind of knowledge not available to other human beings. Instead they think and reason in much the same way as everyone else, but they do so more critically and more systematically. They take less for granted: they ask whether our beliefs are consistent with one another, whether they are supported by evidence, and how, if at all, they can be fitted into one big picture. It is easiest to explain this by taking some examples.

Suppose we were to ask a politician what his goals were; what aims or values the political community he belongs to should be trying to achieve. If he belonged to a contemporary Western society, he would probably come up with a fairly predictable list: law and order, individual liberty, economic growth, full employment, and one or two others. How might a political philosopher respond to this? Well, first of all she would turn the spotlight on the goals themselves and ask which of them were really *ultimate* goals. Take economic growth, for instance. Is this a good thing in itself, or is it only good in so far as it gives people more opportunities to choose from, or makes their lives healthier and happier? Can we assume that further growth is always good, or does there come a point where it no longer contributes to the things that really matter? A similar question might be asked about full employment. Do we value full employment because we believe it is intrinsically valuable for people to engage in paid work, or is it rather that people cannot have a decent standard of living unless they do work? But if the second is true, why not give everyone an income whether they work or not, and make work into a voluntary activity for those who enjoy it?

Our political philosopher will also ask about how the different goals on the politicians' list are related to one another. Politicians very rarely concede that they might have to sacrifice one aim in order to achieve another, but perhaps in reality they do. Take law and order versus individual liberty, for instance. Could our streets not be made safer by limiting individual liberty – for instance by giving the police greater powers to arrest people they suspected were about to engage in criminal acts? If so, which value should have the higher priority? Of course in order to decide that, she would need to say a bit more precisely what individual liberty *means*. Is it simply being able to do whatever you like, or is it doing what you like *so long as you don't harm anyone else*? This makes a big difference to the question being asked.

In raising these questions, and suggesting some answers, political philosophers are not (or needn't be) appealing to any esoteric form of knowledge. They are inviting their readers to reflect on their own political values, and to see which ones they care about most in the final analysis. Along the way they may add in some new pieces of information. For instance, when contemplating the value of economic growth, it is relevant to see how people whose material living standards are very different score in terms of physical indicators such as health and mortality, and psychological indicators such as how satisfied they feel with their lives. Political philosophers therefore need to have a good grasp of social and political science. In earlier periods, they attempted to obtain this primarily by collating such evidence as was available from the historical record about a wide range of human societies, and their various political systems. This evidence was somewhat impressionistic and often unreliable. In this respect political philosophers today can build on more solid empirical foundations by virtue of the huge expansion of the social sciences in the 20th century. But the essential nature of their task remains the same. They take what we know about human societies, and the ways in which they are governed, and then they ask what the best form of government would be, in the light of aims and values that they believe their audience will share. Sometimes this best form of government turns out to be quite close to the form that already exists; sometimes it is radically different.

What I have tried to do in the last few paragraphs is to show how political philosophy can illuminate the way we think about politics without making claims to a special kind of truth that is inaccessible to the ordinary person. There is a related issue here, which is how far the kind of truth political philosophy gives us is universal truth – truth that applies to all societies and in all periods of history. Or is the best we can hope for local knowledge, knowledge that is relevant only to the particular kind of society we live in today?

The answer I want to give is that the agenda of political philosophy changes as society and government change, although some items have stayed on it as far back as our records go. Among these perennial questions are basic questions about politics and political authority that I shall be addressing in the next chapter. Why do we need politics in the first place? What right has anybody to force another person to do something against their will? Why should I obey the law when it does not suit me to? But in other cases, either the questions, or the answers, or both, have changed over time, and we need to see why this is so.

One reason is that changes in society open up possibilities that did not exist before, or alternatively close them off. As an example, think of democracy as a form of government. Almost every political philosopher today – in Western societies at least – takes it for granted that good government must mean some kind of democracy; in one way or another the people must rule (as we shall see in Chapter 3, this leaves plenty of room for argument about what democracy really means in practice). For many centuries beforehand, the opposite view prevailed: good government meant government by a wise monarch, or an enlightened aristocracy, or men of property, or perhaps some combination of these. So are we right and our predecessors simply wrong? No, because democracy seems to need certain preconditions to function successfully: it needs a wealthy and literate population, media of mass communication so that ideas and opinions can circulate freely, a well-functioning legal system that commands people's respect, and so forth. And these conditions did not obtain anywhere until the fairly recent past, nor could they be created overnight (classical Athens is often held up as an exception, but it is important to remember that Athenian 'democracy' encompassed only a minority of the city's population, and rested, as the Greeks themselves recognized, on the work of women, slaves, and resident aliens). So the older philosophers were not wrong to dismiss democracy as a form of government. Even Rousseau, who as we saw earlier was an influential source of democratic ideas, said that it was suitable only for gods and not for men. Given the prevailing conditions, democracy as we understand it today was not a viable form of government.

For another example of the shifting agenda of political philosophy, consider the value we attach today to personal choice. We think people should be free to choose their jobs, their partners, their religious beliefs, the clothes they wear, the music they listen to, and so on and so forth. It is important, we think, that each person should discover or invent the style of life that suits them best. But how much sense would this make in a society where most people, in order to stay alive, are bound to follow in their parents' footsteps, with little choice of occupation, few entertainments, a common religion, and so on? Here other values become much more important. And this is how societies have been for most of human history, so it is hardly surprising that only in the last couple of centuries do we find political philosophies built around the supreme value of personal choice, such as John Stuart Mill's *On Liberty*, which I shall discuss in Chapter 4.

In this book I have tried to strike a balance between the perennial questions of political philosophy and those that have appeared on its agenda only in the fairly recent past, such as the claims of women and cultural minorities discussed in Chapter 6. Striking this balance can be difficult: it is easy to get swept away by the political topics of the moment and lose sight of basic issues that underlie politics everywhere. One remedy is to travel back to Siena and Lorenzetti's frescos and be reminded again that how political authority is constituted can make the difference between plenty and poverty, life and death. This is the starting point of the chapter that follows.

I have also tried to strike a balance between laying out the contrasting positions that have been taken up on these issues, and presenting arguments of my own. My aim is to explain what is at issue when anarchists argue with statists, democrats argue with elitists, liberals argue with authoritarians, nationalists argue with cosmopolitans, and so on, but it would be disingenuous to claim that I am surveying these debates from some entirely neutral, Olympian perspective. One cannot write about political philosophy without doing it as well. So although I have tried not to browbeat the reader into thinking that there is only one plausible answer to some of the most fiercely contested questions of our time, I have not attempted to disguise my sympathies either. Where you disagree with me, I hope you will find the reasons on your side of the argument fairly presented. Of course, I hope even more that you will be convinced by the reasons on *my* side.

Chapter 2
Political authority

If someone were to ask how we govern ourselves today – under what arrangements do we live together in society – the answer must be that we are governed by states that wield unprecedented power to influence our lives. They not only provide us with basic protection against attack on our persons and our possessions, they also regiment us in countless ways, laying down the terms on which we may make our living, communicate with one another, travel to and fro, raise our children, and so on. At the same time they supply us with a huge range of benefits, from health care and education through to roads, houses, parks, museums, sports grounds, and the like. It would not be going too far to say that today we are creatures of the state. Not all states are equally successful in performing these functions, of course, but no one benefits from belonging to a failing state.

Looked at from the perspective of human history, this is a very recent phenomenon. Human societies have usually governed themselves on a much smaller scale. In tribal societies authority might rest in the hands of the village elders, who would meet to settle any disputes that arose among the members of the tribe, or interpret tribal law. When societies emerged on a larger scale, as in China under the Han dynasty or medieval Europe, they still lacked anything that deserved to be called a state. Although supreme authority rested in the hands of the king or the emperor, day-to-day governance was carried out by local lords and their officers. Their impact on people's lives was also much more limited, since they neither attempted to regulate them so closely (except perhaps in matters of religion), nor of course did they attempt to provide most of the goods and services that modern states provide. Political authority was woven into the social fabric in such a way that its existence seemed relatively uncontroversial. The arguments that took place were about who in particular should wield it (by what right did kings rule?), and whether it should be divided between different bodies, for instance between kings and priests.

The emergence of the modern state, however, first in Western Europe, and then almost everywhere else, has meant that the problem of political authority has preoccupied political philosophers for the last 500 years. Here is an institution that claims the right to govern our lives in countless ways. What can justify that claim? Under what circumstances, if any, do states wield legitimate political authority? How far are we as ordinary citizens obliged to obey the laws they make and follow their other dictates? These very basic questions need to be resolved before we can move on in the following chapters to ask how best to constitute the state – what the form of government should be – and what limits should be set to its authority.

When we say that the state exercises political authority, what do we mean? Political authority has two sides to it. On the one side, people generally recognize it *as* authority, in other words as having the right to command them to behave in certain ways. When people obey the law, for instance, they usually do so because they think that the body that made the law has a right to do so, and they have a corresponding duty to comply. On the other side, people who refuse to obey are compelled to do so by the threat of sanctions – law-breakers are liable to be caught and punished. And these two aspects are complementary. Unless most people obeyed the law most of the time because they believed in its legitimacy, the system could not work: to begin with, there would need to be huge numbers of law-enforcement officers, and then the question would arise who should enforce the law on *them*. Equally, those who do keep the law out of a sense of obligation are encouraged to do so by knowing that people who break it are likely to be punished. I do not steal from my neighbour because I respect his right of property. I hope that he respects mine too, but I know that if he doesn't I can call the police to get my property back. So people who comply with authority voluntarily know that they are protected from being taken advantage of by less scrupulous persons.

Political authority, then, combines authority proper with forced compliance. It is neither pure authority, like the authority of the wise man whose disciples follow his instructions without any compulsion, nor pure force, like the force exercised by the gunman who relieves you of your wallet, but a blend of the two. But the question remains, why do we need it? After all political authority, particularly when exercised by a body as powerful as the modern state, imposes a great many unwelcome requirements on us, some of which (like paying taxes) make us materially worse off, but others of which make us do things that we object to morally (like fighting in wars that we oppose). What reply can we give to the anarchist who says that societies can govern themselves perfectly well without political authority, and that the state is essentially a racket run for the benefit of those who hold positions of power?

I shall come back to anarchist alternatives to the state later in the chapter, but first I am going to defend political authority, as others have before me, by asking the reader to imagine life in society without it – with the police, the army, the legal system, the civil service, and the other branches of the state all taken away. What would happen then?

Perhaps the most famous thought-experiment along these lines can be found in Thomas Hobbes's *Leviathan*, published in 1651. Hobbes, as I mentioned in Chapter 1, had experienced the partial breakdown of political authority brought about by the English Civil

War, and the picture he painted of life in its absence was unremittingly bleak. He described the 'natural condition of mankind' without political rule as one of ferocious competition for the necessities of life, leaving people in constant fear in case they should be robbed or attacked, and constantly inclined, therefore, to strike at others first. The result was summed up in a much-quoted passage:

> In such condition, there is no place for Industry; because the fruit thereof is uncertain: and consequently no Culture of the Earth; no Navigation, nor use of the commodities that may be imported by Sea; no commodious Building; no Instruments of moving, and removing such things as require much force; no Knowledge of the face of the Earth; no account of Time; no Arts; no Letters; no Society; and which is worst of all, continuall feare, and danger of violent death; And the life of man, solitary, poor, nasty, brutish, and short.

It is sometimes said that Hobbes reaches this pessimistic conclusion because of a belief that people are naturally selfish or greedy, and will therefore try to grab as much for themselves as they can when unrestrained by political authority. But this misses Hobbes's real point, which is that cooperation between people is impossible in the absence of trust, and that trust will be lacking where there is no superior power to enforce the law. Those things that Hobbes describes as missing in the 'natural condition' are above all things that require numbers of people to work together in the expectation that others will do their part, and in the absence of political authority it is not safe to have any such expectation. If I make an agreement with someone, why should I expect him to keep it, if there is no law to enforce the agreement? And even if he is inclined to keep the agreement, he may wonder the same about me, and decide that it is too risky to do so. In this situation, Hobbes argues, it is only prudent to assume the worst, and take every step you can to secure yourself against the threat of death; and the way to do that, in turn, is to amass as much power relative to other people as you can. At base it is fear of others, born of mistrust, that turns life without political authority into 'a perpetuall warre of every man against his neighbour'.

Was Hobbes's pessimism justified? His critics point out that if we look around us we can find ample evidence of people trusting one another, cooperating with one another, even helping each other with nothing expected in return, without any involvement by the state or any of its branches. A group of neighbours, for instance, may decide together to repair a derelict children's playground, form a team, and divide up the work, each relying on the others to do their bit, without any legal agreement or other means of enforcement. Human nature is not as Hobbes portrayed it. But in a way this misses the point. Although Hobbes probably did have a rather low opinion of human nature (he was once caught out giving money to a beggar, and had to explain that he only did it to relieve his own discomfort at the sight of the beggar), his real point is that in the climate of fear that would follow the breakdown of authority, the kinder, more trusting, side of human nature would be obliterated. And from what we know of human behaviour when people are caught up in civil war and other situations in which their very survival is at stake, he seems to have been right.

We need political authority, then, because it gives us the security that allows us to trust other people, and in a climate of trust people are able to cooperate to produce all those benefits that Hobbes listed as signally lacking in the 'natural condition'. But how can we create authority where it does not exist? Hobbes envisaged everyone gathering together and covenanting with one another to establish a sovereign who would rule them from that day forward; alternatively, they might submit themselves individually to a powerful man, a conquering general for instance. He thought it mattered little who had authority, so long as the authority was unrestricted and undivided. Here we may part company with him. But before looking more closely at how authority should be constituted, we should pause to see whether there is any other way

3. Thomas Hobbes, defender of political authority.

to escape the 'natural condition'. Despite all that Hobbes says, might social cooperation be possible in the absence of political authority?

Anarchists believe that it is indeed possible, and although anarchist voices have always been in a small minority, we should listen to them: as political philosophers we are duty bound to put conventional wisdom to the test, and so we cannot take political authority for granted without exploring the alternatives to it. There are two different directions we might take here: anarchists themselves fall broadly into two camps. One points towards *community*, the other towards the *market*.

The communitarian alternative to political authority takes face-to-face communities as the building blocks that make trust and cooperation between people possible. In a small community where people interact with one another on a daily basis and everyone knows who is a member and who isn't, it is comparatively easy to maintain social order. Anybody who attacks another person, takes their possessions, or refuses to perform his fair share of the community's work, faces some obvious penalties. As news of his behaviour spreads, other people will reprimand him and may refuse to work with him in future. At community meetings he will be denounced and he may even be asked to leave altogether. All this can happen without the malefactor being forced to do anything or being formally punished – that is why we can describe this as an alternative to political authority rather than a form of it. One of the most important human motives is a desire to be accepted and respected by those around you, and in the setting of a small community this makes cooperation possible even if people are not saints.

Communitarian anarchists argue that, in a society made up of communities like this, cooperation will be possible on a much larger scale. Essentially communities will agree to exchange services with one another – they may specialize in producing different kinds of goods for instance – and they will collaborate on projects that need to be carried out on a larger scale, for instance, creating a transport system or a postal service. It is in each community's interest to make these agreements, and the penalty for breaking them is that no one will be willing to cooperate with your community in the future if it proves to be untrustworthy. So once again there is no need for a central authority to tell people what to do, and no need to use coercive force to compel communities to cooperate – the system will effectively be self-policing.

What is wrong with this idyllic picture of life without the state? One major problem is that it relies on small, tight-knit communities as the basis for social order, and although in the past this might have been a reasonable assumption to make, it no longer is today. We live in societies that are highly mobile, both in the sense that people can move around physically quite easily, and in the sense that there is a ready supply of new people to collaborate with, and also, unfortunately, to take advantage of. The anarchist picture is not nonsense, but it works on the assumption that we will interact over time with the same group of people, so that the way we behave becomes common knowledge in the group. It also assumes that the possibility of being excluded from the group is a powerful deterrent to antisocial behaviour. But in a large, mobile society that assumption does not hold. We need, therefore, a legal system that will track down and punish people who injure others, and that allows us to make binding agreements with one another that carry a penalty if we default.

Cooperation between communities is also less straightforward than the anarchist picture supposes. For loyalty to your own community frequently goes along with a fairly intense distrust of others, and agreements may therefore collapse because we over here are not convinced that you over there are contributing your fair share to the project we are supposed to be working on together. And we may disagree about what fairness requires in the first place. Suppose we want to build a society-wide rail network in the absence of a central authority. What share of resources should each community contribute? Should it be so much per head, or should richer communities put in proportionally more? If my community is situated in a remote area that costs much more to connect to the network, should it alone cover the extra cost, or should that cost be shared equally by all communities? There are no easy answers to these questions, and no reason to think that it would be possible for many local communities to come to a voluntary agreement about them. The state, by contrast, can *impose* a solution: it can *require* each person or each community to contribute a certain amount, say through taxation.

Now let us consider the other anarchist alternative to political authority and the state, the one that relies on the economic market. This certainly goes with the grain of the modern world, in so far as the market has proved to be a formidable instrument for allowing people to work together in large numbers. It already supplies us with most of the goods and services we need and want. But could it replace the state?

Market anarchists – sometimes called libertarians – claim that we could contract and pay individually for the services that the state now provides, including crucially for personal protection. In the absence of the state, firms would offer to protect clients and their property, and this would include retrieving property that had been stolen, enforcing contracts, and obtaining compensation for personal injury. So if my neighbour steals something that is mine, instead of calling the (public) police, I would call my protective agency, and they would take action on my behalf against the troublesome neighbour.

But what if the neighbour disputes my claim and calls *his* agency, which may of course be different from mine? If the two agencies cannot agree, libertarians claim, they may refer the case to an arbitrator, who again would charge for her services. After all it is not in the interest of either agency to get into a fight. So there would be a primary market for protective services, and then a secondary market for arbitration services to deal with disputes – unless of course everyone chose to sign up with the same agency (but why would that happen?). And the other services that the state now provides would also be handed over to the market – people would take out health insurance, pay to have their children educated, pay to use toll roads, and so on.

Does this system really do away with political authority? The protective agencies would need to use force to protect their clients' rights. If my neighbour does not hand back the property when it has been established that it rightfully belongs to me, then my agency will send round its heavies to retrieve it. But still, there is no authority proper, because my neighbour is not obliged to recognize my agency – he can always fight back – and I too can change agencies if I dislike the way mine is behaving. So this is genuinely an anarchist alternative to the state. But is it a *good* alternative?

It might look attractive if we thought that the various agencies would all agree to implement the same set of rules to govern property disputes and so forth, and would all consent to independent arbitration in case of dispute. But why should they do this? An agency might hope to win customers by promising to fight on their behalf no matter what – i.e. even if they appeared to be in the wrong by the standards that most people accepted. Once a few agencies like this enter the market, the others would have to respond by taking an equally aggressive line themselves. And this would mean that increasingly disputes would have to be settled by physical force, with the risk to ordinary people of being caught in the cross-fire. We would be slipping back into Hobbes's condition of 'Warre, where every man is Enemy to every man', and in this condition the only rational decision for each person is to sign up with the agency that is likely to win the most fights. But the result would be to create a body with the power and authority to impose the same body of rules on everyone – in other words we would (inadvertently) have recreated the state.

There is another problem with relying on the market to carry out all the functions that states now perform. One of these functions is the provision of what are called 'public goods' – benefits that everyone enjoys and that no one can be excluded from enjoying. These come in many and varied forms – clean air and water, for example, defence against external aggression, access to roads, parks, cultural amenities, media of communication, and so on. These goods are created either by imposing restrictions on people – for example when governments require manufacturers to curb the release of toxic gases into the atmosphere – or by raising taxes and using the revenue to pay for public broadcasting, transport systems, environmental protection, and the like. Could these goods be provided through an economic market? A market operates on the basis that people pay for the goods and services they want to use, and the problem with public goods is precisely that they are provided for everyone whether they pay or not. Of course it is possible that people might contribute voluntarily if they saw the value of the good being provided: old churches that are costly to maintain rely to some extent on visitors who enjoy looking round the church putting money in the box by the door. But it is very tempting to free ride, and in the case of many public goods we may enjoy them almost without realizing it (we don't think, as we get up in the morning, how lucky we are to have breathable air and protection against foreign invasion; we take these things for granted until something goes wrong). So it seems that we need political authority with the power to compel in order to ensure that these goods are provided.

There isn't space here to consider all the ingenious arguments that libertarian anarchists have come up with to show how public goods could be provided through the market, or else by people banding together and agreeing to contribute to their production: in political philosophy there are always more arguments to make. But I hope I have said enough to suggest why neither communities nor markets – important as these are in many areas of human life – can *replace* political authority and its modern embodiment, the state.

4. How anarchists see political authority: Russian cartoon 1900. The text reads, clockwise from the top: we reign over you; we fool you; we eat for you; we shoot you; we rule you.

Much as we may dislike the state when it regulates us, taxes us, conscripts us into its service, and impinges on our lives in many other ways, we could not live well without it. The real choice is not whether to have political authority or not, but what kind of authority to have, and what its limits should be. These are the subjects of the following chapters. But we have not yet quite finished with authority itself. There is still one crucial question that needs to be answered: why should I obey it, when it tells me to do things that I dislike or disapprove of? Political philosophers call this 'the problem of political obligation'.

You might think the question has already been answered, by showing why we need to have political authority. But in fact there is still a gap between recognizing that the British government, say, has a right to make laws and impose taxes, and thinking that I personally am obliged to keep those laws and pay my tax bills. It is not as though my refusal is going to bring the government down, or seriously impede its ability to maintain social order. All states manage to survive a good deal of law-breaking and tax evasion. If I think solely about the consequences of my action, I may well conclude that more good will come from breaking the law – say preventing my local authority from demolishing a historic building by chaining myself to the gates to prevent the bulldozers getting through – or from using the money I would otherwise have paid in tax to support Oxfam. So why should I obey the law?

One reason, of course, is that I am likely to be punished if I don't. But we are looking here for a more principled reason for obeying. Some political philosophers conclude that the problem is insoluble. I should obey the law, they say, only when there are independent reasons to do so, reasons that have nothing to do with the fact that the law emanates from a legitimate authority. But others have tried to provide positive solutions – too many, in fact, for all of them to be considered here. I shall look at just two, the first because it has historically been the most popular, the second because I believe it to be broadly correct.

The first solution claims that we are obliged to obey the law because we have agreed or consented to do so. The appeal of this idea is easy to see. Suppose I go along to my local soccer club and ask to join. When Saturday comes I turn up for the match, but instead of playing by the rules, I insist on picking up the ball and running with it. The club members would no doubt be highly indignant. By joining the club, they would say, I am agreeing to play football by the normal rules, whether or not I have signed an explicit agreement to that effect. My argument that the game is more fun if people are allowed to run with the ball would rightly be ridiculed. This is a *foot*ball club, they would say: anyone who joins implicitly accepts the prevailing rules.

The difficulties begin, however, when we try to transfer this argument from the football club to the state. For generally speaking people do not choose to join states: they are required to obey them whether they like it or not. So in what sense do they give their consent? Hobbes argued that we choose to belong to the state because it is preferable to the state of nature where life, as we saw, is 'nasty, brutish, and short' and it does not matter how the state arises. Even if we submit to a conqueror at the point of a sword, we still consent to his authority, because we do so to escape a worse fate. But this stretches the idea of consent beyond recognition. What made the football club example compelling was the fact that I freely chose to join.

Later writers rejected Hobbes's argument about obligation and consent, and tried to find something other than the mere fact of subjection to the state which could be used to indicate our consent to the law. John Locke, for example, pointed out in his *Second Treatise of Government* (1689) that we all accept benefits from the state, and our acceptance can be treated as a form of consent. In particular, since one of the chief functions of the state is to protect our property, when we acquire it by purchase or inheritance, say, we are also tacitly consenting to the state's jurisdiction over that property, and therefore to its laws. This even applied, Locke thought, to someone who merely took lodgings for a week or travelled on the highway. However the problem again is that we really have little choice about accepting these benefits: we cannot live without property of some kind, even if it is only food and clothing; we cannot escape from the state without travelling the highway to the border. So it still seems to be stretching the idea of consent too far to say that anyone who enjoys state benefits is giving her consent, and obliging herself to obey the law.

More recently, some political philosophers have claimed that when we take part in elections, we agree to comply with the government that emerges and the laws it enacts. This looks more promising: we do at least have a free choice as to whether to vote or not, and there would be no point in holding elections unless people recognized the government that emerged as legitimate. But unfortunately there still seems to be a gap between voting and registering your consent. What if you deeply disagree with both parties, but vote because you think that one is slightly less bad than the other? Or what if you think that although you have in a sense consented to the overall package of policies that the winning party has announced in its manifesto, there are a few items that you find quite repugnant – and you had no chance to vote on these individually? Perhaps the voters' consent can help explain why governments have legitimate authority, but not why individual citizens have an obligation to obey the law.

If we set the consent approach aside, a more promising way of showing that such an obligation exists involves an appeal to fairness or 'fair play'. Again an example is the best way to convey the basic idea. Suppose a group of us are living in a house with a shared kitchen. Every week or so one of the residents tidies the kitchen and gives the pans and the surfaces a really thorough clean. Now everyone else has done the cleaning routine and it is my turn to spend half an hour scrubbing saucepans and mopping worktops. Why ought I to do this? I have benefited from the work the others have put in – I have enjoyed having a clean kitchen to cook my supper in – and so I ought to carry my share of the cost too, in this case the cost of a bit of manual labour. If I don't take my turn, I'll be taking advantage of the other residents, and that's unfair. Notice that we don't need to assume here that I have agreed or consented to take part in the cleaning rota: my obligation stems directly from the fact that I am the beneficiary of a practice that requires each person to contribute in turn.

How does this idea transfer to political obligation? Keeping the law, and complying with political authority more generally, means forgoing opportunities that would otherwise be available to you. Each of us would prefer to do exactly what he pleases, free from the burdens of respecting other people's rights, paying taxes, and observing the traffic laws. Furthermore compliance is a benefit to others. When you pay your taxes, the rest of us benefit from the roads, schools, and hospitals that the taxes are used to pay for. When you stop at the red light, you make it safer for other motorists to cross on green. So it looks as though the person who breaks the law but benefits from the fact that other people are observing it is behaving unfairly in just the same way as the person who uses the kitchen but won't take his turn at cleaning it.

Looks can be deceptive, however. There are at least two difficulties that have to be overcome if the fair play argument is going to justify political obligation. The first is that we have to show that the benefits the state provides really are benefits for everyone. What if the laws protect property, but only some people are property owners, for example? Or what if taxes are being used to fund art galleries and many people care nothing for art? The argument can work, however, so long as the whole *package* of benefits provided by the state makes everyone better off, and so long as the benefits are shared reasonably fairly among all the citizens whose compliance makes the system of authority possible. Perhaps I never visit art galleries, but I do use the football pitch provided free of charge in my local park.

Mention of fairness brings us to the second difficulty. In the kitchen example, I was taking it for granted that each person sharing the house made roughly equal use of the kitchen, and therefore would share the burden of cleaning equally. But what if one person only cooks there once a fortnight? Should she have to clean as often as the rest? Should we say that she does, because after all she *could* use the kitchen more often if she chose, and it is always available in case she needs it? Or should we try to adjust the contribution she is required to make in line with her actual usage? We might call these questions of substantive fairness, and it seems as though the fair play argument works best when it is applied to practices that are substantively fair, in the sense that the costs and benefits of the practice are shared fairly among the individual participants. But if we try to move from the simple kitchen example to society as a whole, we run into difficulties. What would a fair distribution of social costs and benefits look like, given that people have very different needs, abilities, preferences, and so forth? And if, as seems likely, the way that costs and benefits are *actually* distributed in societies today falls very far short of this ideal, can we still say that everyone has an obligation to obey the law in order to maintain a fair practice?

It seems, then, that my preferred solution to the problem of political obligation requires us to tackle the issue of social justice, which we will do in Chapter 5. But suppose for the moment that we are able to show that our society is sufficiently fair that its members do have an obligation to keep the law. Does this mean that they are never justified in breaking it? Or could political obligation be outweighed by other principles? Political philosophers, including Hobbes, have often argued that, without strict obedience to political authority, that authority will crumble into dust. But in practice it seems that states and other forms of political authority can survive and function effectively so long as people are generally (rather than universally) disposed to comply with them, and this opens the door to limited forms of disobedience, especially what has come to be called *civil disobedience* – illegal but non-violent forms of political protest whose purpose is to put pressure on government to change its policies. The argument for civil disobedience is that if a particular law is sufficiently unjust or oppressive, or if the state refuses to listen to the concerns of a minority when making its decisions, this can justify breaking the law if legal forms of protest prove to be ineffective. Political obligation, in other words, need not be binding on all occasions. We can have a general obligation to obey the law, and still be justified in acting illegally in extreme circumstances.

What difference does democracy make here? A common view is that civil disobedience might be an acceptable way of protesting against an authoritarian regime, but in a democratic state, with free speech and the right to protest peacefully, it cannot be justified – political obligation is more stringent here. But this implies that there is something special about democratic political authority that distinguishes it from other forms of political rule. What this special feature might be is the subject of the next chapter.

Chapter 3
Democracy

We have seen why good government, at least in large-scale, modern societies, requires that we establish and maintain a system of political authority. Hobbes, whose lead we followed in showing why political authority is necessary, thought that it was essential to create an absolute sovereign – an undivided source of authority whose writ would be subject to no earthly limitations (Hobbes believed sovereigns still owed obligations to God). It was not essential that this sovereign body be a single person – a monarch – but Hobbes thought this was preferable, because a monarch's will would be constant, and not subject to internal divisions, unlike that of an assembly. But Hobbes's view on this point was challenged from the moment that he wrote by those who thought that to replace the insecurity of the state of nature by an all-powerful monarch able to dispose of his subjects' lives and possessions however he wished was simply going from bad to worse. As John Locke memorably remarked, it assumes that

> Men are so foolish that they take care to avoid what Mischiefs may be done them by *Pole-Cats*, or *Foxes*, but are content, nay think it Safety, to be devoured by *Lions*.

Hobbes's only defence against this criticism was to say that a prudent monarch would wish his subjects to be prosperous, because it was on their prosperity that his own power finally depended. But, looking at the historical record, we might conclude from this that rather few monarchs have been prudent. Political authority is justified because it provides the conditions under which people can live secure and flourishing lives, and we want to be as certain as we can that this is what it does. Trusting everything to an absolute monarch is simply too risky. As an alternative, we might suggest placing authority in the hands of those we know to be wise and virtuous, and to have the interests of the people at heart. This is the argument for aristocracy, which literally means 'the rule of the best', and it was the argument that convinced most political philosophers up until at least the mid-19th century. The problem, however, was to determine what exactly goodness in a ruler amounted to, and then to find some way of selecting those who displayed this quality. This proved difficult to do: in practice aristocracy meant the rule of the well-born, the propertied, or the educated class, depending on time and place. Even if one could show that people drawn from these classes had political skills not possessed by the rest of the population, there was still the problem that they had interests of their own separate from those of the majority – and why believe that they would not pursue these interests at the expense of the common good?

So the case for constituting political authority democratically gathered momentum, and it rested on two basic assumptions: first, that no person was naturally superior to another, so any relations of authority between them stood in need of justification – in other words, each person should enjoy equal political rights unless it could be shown that everyone gained from having inequality; second, that the interests of the people were best safeguarded by making them the final repository of political authority – anyone entrusted with special powers must be accountable to the people as a whole. But this still left it open exactly what role the people as a whole should play in government. Should they be directly involved in legislating, as Rousseau argued in his *Social Contract*, and if so how? Or should they only be involved at one remove, by choosing representatives who would wield authority on their behalf?

5. The Goddess of Democracy facing a portrait of Mao in Tianamen Square, Beijing.

In practice, as we know, those political systems we call democracies give their citizens only a very limited role in government. They are entitled to vote at periodic elections, they are occasionally consulted through a referendum when some major constitutional question has to be decided, and they are allowed to form groups to lobby their representatives on issues that concern them, but that is the extent of their authority. Real power to determine the future of democratic societies rests in the hands of a remarkably small number of people – government ministers, civil servants, and to some extent members of parliament or other legislative assembly – and it is natural to ask why this is so. If democracy is the best way to make political decisions, why not make it a reality by letting the people themselves decide major questions directly?

One answer that is often given at this point is that it is simply impractical for millions of ordinary citizens to be involved in making the huge number of decisions that governments have to make today. If they were to try, not only would government be paralysed, but they would leave themselves no time to do all those other things that most people think are more important than politics. But this answer is not adequate, because it is not difficult to envisage citizens making general policy decisions whose detailed implementation would then be left to ministers and others. The electronic revolution means that it would now be quite easy to ask citizens for their views on a wide range of issues ranging from war and peace through taxation and public expenditure to animal welfare and environmental issues. So why is this done only on those rare occasions when a referendum is called?

The reason is that there is a widespread belief that ordinary people are simply not *competent* to understand the issues that lie behind political decisions, and so they are happy to hand these decisions over to people they regard as better qualified to deal with them. An uncompromising statement of this point of view can be found in Joseph Schumpeter's book *Capitalism, Socialism and Democracy* (1943), where it is argued that the citizen's job is to choose a team of leaders to represent him or her, not to attempt to decide issues directly. Schumpeter claims that whereas in economic transactions, for instance, people experience the results of their decisions directly – if they buy a defective product, they soon discover their mistake – in the case of political decisions there is no such feedback mechanism, and as a result people lose touch with reality and behave irresponsibly.

> Thus the typical citizen drops down to a lower level of mental performance as soon as he enters the political field. He argues and analyses in a way which he would readily recognize as infantile within the sphere of his real interests. He becomes a primitive again.

This is strong stuff, and what it really entails is that the best we can hope for is what is sometimes called 'elective aristocracy', where all that can be asked of the ordinary citizen is that she should be able to recognize people who are competent to make decisions on her behalf (and to vote them out of office if they prove not to be). Whatever its other virtues, such a system hardly matches the democratic ideal that political authority must rest in the hands of the people as a whole. So what can we say in response to Schumpeter's scepticism? Let us look more closely at what is involved in reaching political decisions.

A political decision essentially requires a political *judgement* about what ought to be done in circumstances where there are several options open and there is disagreement about which option is best. What are the elements that go into such a judgement? First of all there is factual information about what will happen if one or other option is chosen. What effect will a particular tax increase have on the economy, for instance? Second, there is information about what the people who will be affected by the decision actually prefer. Suppose the tax increase is being considered in order to fund new sports facilities, say, how many people actually want these facilities, and how much do they want them? Third, there are questions of moral principle. Is it *fair* that everyone should be taxed to pay for sports facilities, or should the cost be borne by those who are going to use them?

In most cases, making a political judgement will involve all of these three elements, although the mix will vary from case to case. Some issues are primarily technical, so that once we can agree about the factual questions at stake, the decision will be fairly straightforward. Before we license a new drug, for instance, we will want to know that it has been properly tested and shown to be safe, but once that has been done, it is a routine matter to give the green light. In other cases, questions of moral principle are central. Take the debate about whether the death penalty should be adopted or retained for certain crimes. Factual information is relevant here – how effective a deterrent will the death penalty prove to be for crimes of these kinds, how likely is it that innocent people will be convicted? – but the key issue, for most people, is whether we are morally permitted to take the life of another human being by way of punishment.

The hardest judgements to make are on questions that involve all three elements at once. Consider the current debate in Britain about whether fox-hunting should be permitted or banned. Factual questions are relevant here: how much does fox-hunting contribute to control of the fox population? What would be the effect of an outright ban on the rural economy? So also are questions of preference: how much does it matter to those who now hunt foxes that they should continue to do this rather than, say, chasing hounds along aniseed trails? And do other country-dwellers want hunting to continue, or are they fed up with horses and hounds trampling their fields and damaging their fences? And finally there are the moral issues: does personal liberty include the right to hunt foxes? Or do foxes and other animals have rights that include the right not to be killed? Most people, in reaching a decision, would want to take all of these questions into account, and that is why it is hard to form a rational judgement on the issue. In practice, of course, people do have strong opinions on issues such as this, but perhaps this just shows that Schumpeter's disparaging remarks about the ordinary citizen's level of competence on political questions are fully justified.

But now let us ask whether the people who are chosen to represent them can be expected to do any better, taking each element of political judgement in turn. One of the great difficulties that beset political decision-making in contemporary societies is that many judgements require factual information that only those who are really expert on the subject in question can provide. This is obviously true when scientific matters are at stake, but the same applies in the case of many economic and social issues, where the problem is to determine what are the likely effects of a proposed new law or policy. Would legalizing cannabis increase or decrease the number of those who end up taking heroin and other hard drugs, for instance? The answer to such questions is far from obvious, and elected politicians and civil servants in general have no more expertise in answering them than the rest of us. Like us, they have to rely on the opinions of those who do have some expertise, and where those opinions differ, they have to make a judgement about who is more reliable. So far, there is no reason to think that an elective aristocracy will make better judgements than the general public.

The next element is to discover what people's preferences are, and how strong they are, and here, you may well think, democracy has a decisive advantage. For when decisions are taken democratically everyone has a chance to contribute, and so the views and preferences of people from different social classes, different ethnic and religious backgrounds, and so forth, will all be heard, whereas the political class who govern us today are predominantly white, male, and middle class. Of course members of parliament, and other legislators, are supposed to listen to their constituents' views, but in reality they enjoy a very high degree of independence – in so far as they are under pressure to vote in one way rather than another, it comes from their party, not from the people who elected

6. One way to invigorate democracy: politicians beware!

them. So if we want political decisions to respect the preferences of those who are going to be subject to them, shouldn't we listen to the people as a whole rather than to a small, socially unrepresentative minority?

But before jumping to that conclusion, there is a complication we need to consider. Suppose that we have an issue where the majority favours one policy, but the minority, which favours a different policy, cares much more strongly about it than the majority. Cases of this kind occur quite often. The fox-hunting debate may be a good example. Most people hold fairly negative views about fox-hunting, even if they do not hold strong moral views about the rights of animals. They see it as an archaic, snobbish, and generally distasteful spectacle; given the chance, they would vote to ban it. The fox-hunters themselves are a small minority, but they mostly feel very strongly that they should be allowed to continue hunting. It is an important social event in many rural communities, and people's livelihoods depend on it. A political judgement about fox-hunting ought to consider not only the *number* of preferences on either side, but also the *strength* of those preferences. It does not seem right that a lukewarm majority should in all cases override a passionate minority.

Why might elected representatives be likely to make a better judgement than the general public on issues like this? One reason is that they are more likely to be lobbied by members of the minority who feel strongly about the issue. They may be persuaded when they see the strength of feeling on that side of the argument, or they may just be concerned not to lose votes at the next election. Moreover minorities can join forces, agreeing to support one another's demands, so that taking several issues together a majority coalition can emerge. This picture of representative democracy is sometimes called pluralism, and it rests on the assumption that people will be moved to form groups to defend their strongly felt interests and preferences, and that decision-makers will respond to the activities of such groups, which besides lobbying might involve demonstrating or even perhaps engaging in illegal forms of protest.

There is certainly some truth in the pluralist picture, but political scientists have tended to be sceptical. For group pressure depends not only the number of people who care about an issue, and how much they care, but also how well organized and resourced the group is. And that gives a built-in advantage to certain interests, most notably business interests, who can hire persuasive advocates to lobby on their behalf – possibly even enlist elected representatives directly – and also plausibly threaten dire consequences if their demands are not met. Under a representative system, then, minorities are indeed listened to, but by no means all minorities to the same extent.

Compare now what might happen if the whole public had to vote on some issue where the majority and the minority had different preferences. There would be no central point at which lobbying activities could be directed, so any group would have to rely on direct contact between its members and as many of the public as they were able to reach. Groups with plenty of resources might be able to use these to run media campaigns – though this could be limited in the same way as election expenditures are limited in many democracies today. They would have much less influence in this direct version of democracy than they do under a representative system. So in general we can say that minority groups would have to rely more on persuasion and less on power and influence under a system of this kind. How they fared would depend primarily on whether members of the majority were willing to listen to their concerns and respond by changing their own views, perhaps by finding a compromise. I shall say more shortly about the crucial role that discussion has to play in democratic decision-making. But before that we need to consider the third element in political judgement, the moral element.

Moral principles are involved in almost all political decisions, not only those involving so-called 'moral issues' such as abortion or the legalization of homosexuality. Typically the question is whether a proposed piece of legislation treats all individuals or all groups fairly, or whether it infringes any of their rights. Do members of the political class have any deeper knowledge of the relevant principles than ordinary citizens? It is difficult to argue that they do: there are no moral experts, it is often said. In fact, there is likely to be a large measure of agreement on the basic principles that should govern political life in a democratic society. So there is no reason to think that if citizens were asked to decide issues directly, they would make a worse job of it on moral grounds than the people they currently choose to represent them.

But can we really separate these three elements of political judgement, or is political expertise precisely a matter of being able to *combine* relevant factual information, knowledge of citizens' interests and preferences, and moral principle, to find the best solution to a political dilemma? There is certainly something in this challenge. Political decisions are often hard to make: they may require mastering some complex information, or weighing up two finely balanced moral arguments. People who have to make them frequently get better at doing so. But this is not because they have some special inborn capacity denied to the rest of us. There is no reason to think that ordinary members of the public, given the time and the information that they need to think carefully about a problem, would not perform as well. There is some evidence to bear this out: *citizens' juries* are small committees whose members are randomly selected from the general public, formed in order to discuss and make recommendations on issues such as health policy and transport strategy. They call expert witnesses to provide information, listen to advocates representing different points of view, and debate the issues among themselves before coming to a verdict. Observers have been struck by how serious and thoughtful their discussions are, and how reasonable their conclusions.

So how are we to explain the low levels of political knowledge and political interest that most citizens in democratic societies show when interviewed or surveyed? Typically they cannot name leading politicians, cannot explain how the main parties differ on policy issues, and so on. One explanation is that democracy as currently practised gives people very little incentive to acquire political knowledge or skill. All they are asked to do is to make a party choice once every four or five years, and you do not need to know much about politics in order to make a decision of that kind. Understanding the finer details of policy is usually irrelevant. So we face a chicken and egg problem. It would be risky to ask the general public to make major policy decisions unless they have the skills and information to make good judgements, but they have no incentive to acquire these unless they are given significant decisions to make.

Should we worry about the fact that our democracy remains incomplete so long as the political role of ordinary citizens is largely confined to voting at elections, plus intermittent activity when some particular interest of theirs is at stake (such as responding to a planning proposal to put a new road or housing development in their back yard)? I think we should. Our word 'idiot' comes from the Greek *idiotes* which was the term used to describe someone who lived an entirely private existence and took no part in the public life of the city. Most of us today are idiots, then, inasmuch as we fail to exercise our political intelligence. Rousseau thought that handing over political authority entirely to elected representatives was a pernicious modern practice:

> The people of England deceive themselves when they fancy they are free; they are so, in fact, only during the election of members of parliament: for, as soon as a new one is elected, they are again in chains, and are nothing. And thus, by the use they make of their brief moments of liberty, they deserve to lose it.

Even if we think Rousseau exaggerates here, we ought to be concerned that most citizens in contemporary democracies are too apathetic even to keep an effective watch over the activities of their elected leaders. We need to develop forms of participation, either at local level, or through selecting members of the public at random to sit on citizens' juries and other such bodies, that give everyone the experience of active citizenship. Experience that is gained in this way raises people's competence generally and makes them more likely to take a continuing interest in political affairs. Democracy, we discover, is not an all-or-nothing matter, but a continuing struggle to give the people as a whole final authority over the affairs of the state.

But now we must return to the unresolved issue of the majority and the minority. For although in a shorthand way we think of democracy as 'government by the people', in reality when decisions have to be made it is usually the majority which decides them (indeed elections are often won by parties who are supported by *less* than a majority of voters). Since it is very unlikely that there will be unanimous agreement on the best policy to be adopted, majority voting seems unavoidable as a way of making decisions, but what are we to say about those who end up on the losing side?

7. Jean-Jacques Rousseau, philosopher of democracy.

It might at first seem as though they have no legitimate complaint to make: after all their votes were counted equally with those of the majority, and to give them any *greater* weight would violate the idea of political equality that as we saw lies behind democracy itself. But that is not the end of the matter. There are two circumstances in particular in which a minority may feel that majority rule *violates* political equality. One we have already encountered: the case where those who vote with the majority are affected much less by the decision, or have fewer interests at stake, than those who form the minority. Although heads have been counted equally, it appears as though preferences or interests have not. The second circumstance is one where one group finds itself in a minority repeatedly when votes are taken. Imagine a rackets club which has a larger number of keen tennis players and a smaller number of equally keen squash players, and imagine that every time a vote is taken on whether to spend money upgrading the tennis or the squash courts, the squash players lose. We might think that this arrangement does not treat each member equally, and is therefore less democratic than one where the squash players get their way from time to time. In other words, we have the problem of the *intense* minority and the problem of the *persistent* minority.

How might these problems be addressed in a democracy? There are broadly two approaches that we can take. The first is to design a constitution that limits the scope of majority rule in such a way as to protect minorities. For instance, the constitution may contain a list of rights that every citizen must enjoy: a proposed law or policy decision that would infringe one of these rights will be thrown out as unconstitutional – there has therefore to be a special authority, usually a constitutional court, that is given the power to decide whether a measure that is being considered, or has been provisionally adopted, is in breach of the constitution. Any minority then has the assurance that whatever the majority decides cannot violate one of their basic rights as laid down in the constitution.

Arrangements such as this are often criticized as undemocratic, because they give a small committee of judges, for instance, the right to block the expressed will of the majority of citizens. But it is not difficult to envisage the constitution itself being adopted by a democratic procedure, and most real-world constitutions make provision for amendment, usually requiring more than just a simple majority of voters to support an amendment if it is to pass. Why would people vote for a constitution that restricted their power to make majority decisions in future? They might well do so because they wanted certain of their rights protected, and could not be sure that they might not find themselves as part of an unpopular minority. Take religious freedom as an example. Anyone with religious beliefs wants to be sure that she can practise her religion safely, even if the majority in her society is strongly opposed to the particular religion she believes in. It is not easy to predict which religions might incur the wrath of the majority in future, so by having a right to freedom of worship included in the constitution, she can get that security.

Another constitutional device to protect minorities is to create separate constituencies to decide different sets of issues. This happens, for example, in federal systems, where regions or provinces are given the power to legislate on issues that are particularly relevant to their inhabitants, with other decisions being reserved for the central government. But the separate constituencies need not be territorially based. Let us go back again to the example of the rackets club whose squash players get a raw deal. An obvious solution to the problem is to create two subcommittees, one to look after the tennis courts and the other the squash facilities, and to give part of the club's annual budget to each. Minorities are protected here by being turned into majorities on the issues that matter most to them.

It would be naïve, however, to think that all minority problems can be solved by one or other of these constitutional devices. The issue of fox-hunting reveals this only too clearly. Those who want to hunt foxes cannot defend themselves simply by appealing to their

51

constitutional rights, because it is very unlikely that any constitution will incorporate an unlimited right to hunt animals. In the next chapter I shall be looking in more detail at how we might try to establish a realm of personal freedom that governments have no right to infringe, but it is fairly easy to see that hunting rights are not going to be included in that story. The hunting of animals is surely a legitimate matter for majority decision, because both animal welfare and the protection of endangered species are issues that potentially concern everyone. Nor can the strongly held views of the fox-hunters be addressed by saying that fox-hunting is an issue over which they and they alone should have the power to decide. There are obviously far too many conflicting interests at stake for the decentralized solution that worked in the rackets club case to work fairly here.

So although constitutional devices are an important way of ensuring that minorities do not suffer at the hands of the majority, a democratic system that aims to treat every citizen equally has to go further. It has to try to ensure that the majority takes the concerns of the minority properly into account before reaching a final decision, even in cases where basic rights are not at issue. The key to this is public discussion, where both sides listen to the other's point of view, and try to find a solution that as far as possible is acceptable to both. In other words, the people who form the majority do not simply vote for the solution that they most preferred prior to the debate. Instead they try to form a judgement after listening to the arguments made on the other side. Sometimes they can find a general principle that both sides can agree to and that provides a way forward.

But why should the majority behave like this? Usually the eventual solution involves the people on that side of the debate giving up part of what they had originally wanted – for instance, people who started off wishing to ban fox-hunting entirely might accept, after hearing the arguments, that hunting should be allowed to continue provided it is properly regulated. But if you have numbers on your side, why retreat in that way? There are two reasons. One is simply respect for your fellow-citizens. You may disagree with them deeply on the particular issue that is on the table, but their voices are supposed to count equally, in a democracy, and so you must listen to them before you decide – and if possible find a solution that takes account of what they say (there are some issues over which no accommodation is possible, but these are actually quite rare: even in a case like abortion, for instance, there are other possibilities besides an outright ban and making abortions freely available on demand). The other reason is that next time round you may find yourself in a minority, and then you will want those on the other side to take *your* concerns into account. In other words you have an interest in promoting a democratic culture in which majorities do not simply ride roughshod over minorities, but try to consider their interests fairly when reaching decisions.

Democracy, it turns out, is a demanding business. It requires people to take an interest in political issues that are often complex and seemingly remote from their daily lives, and it requires them to exercise self-restraint when deciding those issues – in particular by not trampling on minority groups even when they have the power to do so. It can be hard to resist the siren voices that tell us that we are better off leaving political decisions to those we have chosen to represent us. But unless we resist – unless we hold fast to the idea that political authority must finally rest with the whole body of citizens – we will end up, as Locke warned, being devoured by the lions who rule us.

This discussion of democracy has also raised three further issues that will occupy us in the chapters that follow. One is whether there is a sphere of personal freedom that should be protected against the intrusion even of democratic government. Another is whether some minority groups should be given *special* rights, over and above the constitutional rights that all citizens should enjoy, to ensure that they are treated fairly. And the third is about the conditions under which democracy is possible at all – specifically about when people will trust one another sufficiently for them to respect a democratic constitution, and be willing to discuss and decide issues in an atmosphere of mutual respect. In the next chapter I deal with the first of these questions.

Chapter 4
Freedom and the limits of government

If we imagine our Siennese painter, Ambrogio Lorenzetti, transported in a time machine to the present day, and asked for his opinion of the political philosophy contained in this book, I believe he would find much that has been said up to now familiar and broadly acceptable. He would probably think I had given anarchist ideas more space than they deserve, and he would find it extraordinary that anyone should have moral objections to hunting foxes. But on the nature of political authority, on the need for rulers to be responsible to the whole body of citizens, and on what good political judgement requires, we would (I hope) find ourselves in broad agreement. Yet Lorenzetti would find the chapter that now begins much more puzzling. It is about the question whether there is a realm of human freedom that must be kept beyond the reach of politics – whether there are areas of human life in which government must categorically not intervene. This idea, which is a central element in the dominant political ideology of our age, liberalism, had not appeared when Lorenzetti was painting. Of course Lorenzetti's good government left its people a considerable amount of liberty: they were largely left free to farm, to trade, to hunt, and so on. But this was not a matter of principle, more a matter of the limited capacity of governments to intervene in these areas of daily life.

The idea of limited government took shape over several centuries, and the first impetus came from the religious conflicts that followed the European Reformation of the 16th century. When the monopoly of the Roman Catholic Church over the religious life of Christian societies was broken, the initial response was that each political community should have its own established religion, Catholic or Protestant. But the multiplication of Protestant sects gave rise to a demand for religious toleration: within certain limits, each person was entitled to find his own path to God, and the state had no business interfering with this quest. With the further passage of time, the claim for religious freedom expanded to become a wider claim for personal freedom – for each person's right to choose his own beliefs and his own way of life so long as these choices did not impinge directly on anyone else. In particular the Romantic movement of the late 18th and early 19th centuries bequeathed to all later generations the idea that each person is a unique individual who can find true fulfilment only if she is allowed to choose for herself how she should live, and this requires the greatest possible space to try out new and unconventional ways of living – new occupations, new forms of artistic expression, new ways of conducting personal relationships, and so forth. As John Stuart Mill put it in his classic text *On Liberty* (whose practical proposals we shall come to later):

> There is no reason that all human existence should be constructed on some one or some small number of patterns. If a person possesses any tolerable amount of common sense and experience, his own mode of laying out his existence is the best, not because it is the best in itself, but because it is his own mode. Human beings are not like sheep; and even sheep are not indistinguishably alike.

Because individual freedom is of such great value, liberals argued, governments must be prohibited from interfering with it, no matter how well they are constituted. Good government is not enough: even the best-constructed and best-intentioned government will be tempted to intrude in areas in which individual liberty ought to be sacrosanct. This is the idea that Lorenzetti would have found so strange, and that I shall explore in the present chapter.

There are two central questions that we need to ask. First, what exactly is the freedom we are talking about? What does it mean to say that someone is free to do this or that, or live in one way or another? Second, what are the limits of individual freedom? What should happen when my freedom comes into conflict with other political goals, including the freedom of everyone else? Is there a principled way to decide this?

Let us begin then with freedom itself, an elusive idea that has filled the pages of many books of political philosophy. As a first shot, let us say that a person's freedom depends on the number of options open to her, and on her capacity to make a choice between them. Someone who has a choice between ten different jobs has greater freedom than someone who only has two to choose between. Of course the quality of the options matters too: you may think that having two good jobs to choose between gives you more freedom than having ten lousy ones, particularly if the lousy ones are all rather similar (street cleaner, office cleaner, toilet cleaner, etc.). So rather than 'number of options' we should perhaps say 'extent of options' where this takes into account both how different the options are, and how valuable they are. As to the second clause, 'capacity to choose', we need this because someone might be presented with options but for one reason or another not be able to exercise a genuine choice between them. For instance suppose someone offers you the choice of going to see one or other of two plays this evening, but only tells you their titles, neither of which means anything to you at all. You can pick a play at random, but you cannot choose in the sense of deciding which play you would most like to see. Or again suppose that someone is completely under her mother's thumb and always does what mother suggests. She is offered various jobs, but invariably takes the one that her mother recommends. From one point of view she has the freedom to choose her employment, but from another point of view she hasn't.

So we can say that freedom has an external and an internal aspect: it depends on whether the world is arranged in such a way that someone has many doors open to him, but it also depends on whether he is able to choose, genuinely, which door to pass through. But now we need to dig a bit deeper to see what it means for a door to be open, and what it means to make a genuine choice.

When can we say that an option is available for someone to choose? Let us turn this around and ask when an option is *not* available. The most clear-cut case is one where it has been made physically impossible for the person in question to pursue that option. Someone who has been tied up or thrown in gaol has very little freedom because he is physically prevented from doing nearly all of the things that he might otherwise do. Some political philosophers, including our old friend Hobbes, have argued that it is *only* physical impediments that restrict people's freedom. But to most people this seems a very narrow view. We generally think that options become unavailable when sanctions of various kinds are attached to them. Laws, in particular, restrict the freedom of those who are subject to them, because a penalty is applied to law-breakers. There is nothing to prevent me physically from driving above the speed limit or smashing the windows in my neighbour's house, but if I do these things I am liable to be caught and punished, so I am not free to do them. The same applies to threats issued by private individuals. If someone threatens to beat me up if he catches me talking to his girlfriend again, then (assuming the threat is meant seriously), that option is no longer open to me.

Physical prevention and sanctions are generally accepted as barriers that reduce freedom. Much more controversy arises in cases where people may be deterred from pursuing options because of the cost of doing so, where the cost does not take the form of a punishment or some other sanction. As the question is sometimes put, is a penniless person free to dine at an expensive restaurant – the Ritz, for instance? Do we say 'No' because in reality there is no way that person can eat at the Ritz (at least without suffering some fairly dire consequences when it is discovered that he has no money)? Or do we say 'Yes' because the only thing preventing him is his lack of resources, not any intention on the part of the Ritz's owners or anyone else to stop him from eating there? This is more than just a philosophical question, because how we answer it affects the way we think about the relationship between government and freedom. Among the policies pursued by governments are those that transfer resources from one set of hands to another – typically from better off to worse off people. We would like to know whether this increases the freedom of the recipients, or decreases the freedom of the contributors, or neither, or both.

So let's consider some examples in which people cannot do things that they would otherwise choose to do because of the cost. Should we say that once the cost reaches a certain point people are no longer free? This is too simple: compare someone on a modest income who cannot buy a holiday that costs £10,000 with someone on the same income who needs an operation to relieve a painful (though not disabling) condition that is only available privately for £10,000. Why do we say that the second person is not free to have the operation he needs, whereas in the first case we typically use different language – he is free to have the holiday, but he simply cannot afford it, we might say? Why does the language of freedom come naturally in the second case but not the first? Expensive holidays are luxury items whose distribution can reasonably be left to the economic market, where people make choices over how much they earn and how they spend their income. Whether or not the person we are considering could actually have raised £10,000 by working longer hours, changing jobs, or cutting back on other expenditure – that may be in dispute – we know for certain that nobody was under any obligation to provide him with the holiday. In contrast, the state has an obligation to ensure that everyone has access to adequate health care, whether through a public health service or by regulating the health insurance market so that everyone can buy suitable cover. So if someone is left facing a £10,000 bill for an operation that she needs, responsibility for this lies with the state, which has failed in its obligation. Whether the cost of taking an option is a restriction of freedom depends not just

59

8. A controversial view of liberty, 1950.

on how big the cost is, but on how the cost arose and whether anyone else can be held responsible for its existence.

The commonly held view that the more governments do, the less freedom people have, is therefore mistaken. Governments do sometimes restrict freedom, sometimes justifiably, sometimes not (seat-belt legislation, for example, restricts the freedom of car-users, but most people would agree that it is justified by the lives it saves). But at other times government action can increase freedom, by giving people options that they would not have otherwise because of the cost. We need to look at particular policies, to see whether in opening options up they are closing down other ones that are more important. Unfortunately much political rhetoric about 'the free society' never gets down to this level of detail. Political philosophers, who ask exactly what we mean when we say that a person is or is not free to pursue a particular option, can help us make better-informed and more nuanced judgements about the relationship between government and personal freedom. This is a good illustration of my argument in Chapter 1 about the value of thinking philosophically about the political issues of the day.

Government can do less directly about the internal aspect of freedom, a person's capacity to make genuine choices among the options open to her. This is sometimes called 'positive liberty' as distinct from the 'negative liberty' of having options that are not blocked by external factors. These two kinds of liberty have been contrasted with each other, as they were by the political philosopher Isaiah Berlin in a famous lecture called 'Two Concepts of Liberty'. Berlin wanted to highlight the dangers in 'positive liberty' which he believed could be used in such a way as to justify authoritarian or totalitarian regimes, like Stalin's Soviet Union, which gave their subjects very little 'negative liberty'. But I believe it is more fruitful to see them as complementary, and I gave examples earlier to suggest why we should be concerned about genuine choice as well as about the availability of options. But how are we to know when a choice is genuine? This is more difficult to decide.

It may help once again to approach this question from the opposite angle, by asking when choices are obviously *not* genuine. A fairly clear-cut example is provided by people who are in the grip of a compulsion or an addiction – for instance kleptomaniacs who simply cannot help shoplifting when the opportunity arises, or drug addicts who will go to any lengths to get the next fix. People in this position act on their strongest desire at the moment of decision, but when they stand back and reflect, they know that these are not the desires they want to have. If they could push a button to get rid of the compulsion or addiction, they would. Their decision to grab the shirt or inject the heroin is not a genuine choice because it is motivated by an urge that the individual involved would rather not have.

A different example occurs when a person's choices are determined by an outside force, like the girl who always does what her mother tells her. Although the person concerned appears content with her decisions – there is no inner struggle as there often is in the case of the compulsive or the addict – we feel that the decisions are not really hers. Genuine choice requires a certain kind of independence; a free person must ask herself 'what do I really want or really believe' and be able to reject second-hand answers. People lose their freedom, in this sense, when the social pressure on them to conform to prevailing conventions or prevailing beliefs becomes so intense that they are unable to resist. Religion and political ideology can both have this effect.

How can we promote this inner freedom, the capacity to make genuine choices? One way is to expose people to a wide range of alternatives, so that they are less likely to take it for granted that any one set of beliefs, or any one way of life, must be the right one (conversely religious sects and political regimes that want to control their members' choices go to great lengths to ensure that they do not get to see or experience anything that deviates from their approved way of living). So a government that wanted to promote freedom to choose could do so by encouraging social diversity – by exposing people to new ways of living, new forms of culture, and so on. One practical manifestation of such a policy would be an education system that encouraged children to think critically about the beliefs and values they have inherited from their parents or imbibed from their social network, and at the same time exposed them to other faiths and other cultural values by drawing children from different communities together in common schools. But unlike external freedom, internal freedom cannot be guaranteed. Some people are independent-minded by nature; others are born conformists. All that politics can do is to provide more favourable conditions for those who want to choose their own path in life to do so.

So far I have tried to explain what freedom is and why it is valued so highly in contemporary societies. Now I want to begin to explore its limits. That individual freedom must be limited in various ways should be self-evident: the freedom of each person must be restricted to allow everyone to enjoy (external) freedom to the same extent, but beyond that there are many legitimate social goals whose pursuit involves placing limits on what individuals may do. To protect the natural environment, for instance, we have to prevent people dumping litter, poisoning the air with exhaust gases, turning wildlife habitats into housing estates, and so forth. We balance freedom against other values, and sometimes freedom has to give way. But how far should this balancing go? Is there a sphere of personal freedom that we are never justified in infringing, no matter how good the consequences of restricting freedom might appear to be?

John Stuart Mill, whose essay *On Liberty* I have already cited, believed that there was indeed such a sphere within which liberty should be inviolable. He argued that when a person's actions were 'self-regarding', meaning that they caused no harm to the interests of anyone except possibly the person himself, they should never be interfered with. Mill thought that this principle would justify freedom of thought and expression, and the personal freedom to

9. Isaiah Berlin, the most widely read philosopher of liberty in the 20th century.

live in the way one wanted – how to dress, what to eat and drink, what cultural activities to pursue, what sexual relationships to have, what religion to follow, and so on. (These ideas are familiar to us now, but when Mill wrote, in the mid-Victorian period, they were regarded as radical, indeed even as shocking.) But is it possible to draw the line that Mill wanted to draw? Are there really any actions that are certain to cause no harm other than to the person who performs them?

Mill acknowledged that people might well be *offended* by behaviour that he would classify as self-regarding – by outrageous dress, unusual sexual practices, militant atheism, and so on. But he argued that being offended by something is not the same as being harmed by it. Harm is a matter of being attacked or threatened, having your property destroyed, or your economic position worsened, and in Mill's eyes this was something that could be established objectively. Offence, by contrast, depends on the personal beliefs and attitudes of the person offended – you may be offended by homosexuality, or rap music, but that is because according to your personal scale of values these activities are wrong or unacceptable, my reaction may be quite different. Mill thought it was perfectly in order for those who found other people's behaviour offensive to avoid the offenders, or indeed to try to persuade them to change their ways, but what they were not permitted to do was to prevent, by law or other means, the behaviour in question.

But we can ask whether offence and harm can be so easily separated. Suppose that a woman works in an office or factory where most employees are male, and who insist on displaying large posters of naked women that she finds offensive. As a result, she dislikes being at work and may even decide to leave. In an obvious sense, she is being harmed by the apparently self-regarding behaviour of the male employees. Another example is provided by so-called 'hate speech' – vicious remarks directed in public at members of ethnic or religious minorities, which may drive them away from schools, colleges, or workplaces, or at least make them feel very uncomfortable about being there. Again it seems that behaviour that is immediately simply offensive may indirectly cause harm, so we have a choice: either we can expand our idea of harm to include these cases, in which case the sphere of self-regarding actions will shrink, or we stick to the original idea that only behaviour that is directly harmful can be interfered with, and say that people should be left free to express themselves even when other people find the form of expression deeply offensive.

Three things are particularly worth noting about the examples we have just considered. First, it is not just a matter of personal idiosyncrasy that the behaviour is found offensive. Whatever we think ourselves about nude posters, we should be able to understand why many women find them offensive. It is very different from, say, objecting to someone pinning a David Beckham poster over their desk because you support a rival football team. Second, the offence is not avoidable except by a large change in the victim's behaviour, for instance giving up the job or leaving the college. This contrasts with the case where I am offended by the posters on the walls of my neighbour's living room – which I can avoid by keeping out of his house – or by the opinions expressed in a racist newspaper, which I need not buy. Third, the offensive behaviour itself has little or no positive value to set against the distress that it causes: it is not an essential part of anyone's idea of the good life that they must be able to gaze at naked women while they work or that they should shout abuse at blacks or Muslims. (I don't deny that a few people may want, quite badly, to do these things; the question is, what is lost if they are prevented?) Although freedom of expression is important, not all expression should count for the same. It is very important that people should be able to worship freely, engage in political debate, express themselves artistically, and so on; very unimportant that they should be able to display posters at work or shout crude racist slogans.

So instead of Mill's simple principle – that self-regarding behaviour may never be interfered with – we may find that we need to make more complex judgements, weighing the value of different kinds of behaviour against the costs they may impose on others, and the ease with which those costs could be avoided.

I turn now to a different problem for Mill's principle: forms of behaviour that have no immediate effect on anyone but the person herself may still have long-term consequences for other people because they make that person less able to contribute to society, or create costs that others have to pay. For instance, someone who becomes an alcoholic may be unable to hold a steady job; someone who smokes heavily, even if only in their own home, increases their chance of getting cancer or heart disease, and therefore of needing medical treatment at public expense. The question, therefore, is whether we should count these activities as purely self-regarding, and entitled to protection in the name of individual freedom.

Mill considered the example of alcoholism and argued that drinking ceased to be purely self-regarding in two cases: when the person involved had taken on a job or a commitment that could not be performed properly under the influence of alcohol, and when the person was liable to engage in acts of violence while drunk. But if the effect of drinking was simply to render the person less able to make a social contribution than he otherwise might, society had no right to prevent it. Children could be taught about their social responsibilities and warned about the dangers of alcohol and so forth. But for adults, preserving freedom was of paramount importance even if society as a whole suffered as a result.

One reason why we may hesitate to follow Mill here is that the state has taken on a far wider range of responsibilities to its citizens since the time that he wrote, and so it has to cover the costs incurred by much more apparently self-regarding activity. When Mill wrote *On Liberty* there was no public health service, no national system of education or of income support for the poor, no public housing, and so on. To a very large extent, those who damaged their health or made themselves unfit for work had to bear the costs themselves, or had to apply to local charities, who were entitled to impose conditions on those they supported. The question is whether Mill's principle still makes sense against the background of a welfare state, funded by taxation, that is committed to providing everyone with a minimum level of income, education, health care, and housing. In this context, should people have enforceable social responsibilities both to contribute and to avoid becoming unnecessarily dependent on welfare services?

This is one of the most controversial issues in politics today, and one reason that we may find ourselves eventually agreeing with Mill is that there seems no obvious stopping place once we abandon his principle of liberty. For instance, should the state require people to eat a healthy diet? Should it force them to take regular exercise? Should it prevent them from engaging in dangerous sports? Any of these measures would significantly cut the cost of public health care, but we may none the less think that they involve an intolerable degree of intrusion in private life. In which case, we may conclude that the state can legitimately require participants to insure themselves when they go mountaineering or engage in extreme sports; and that it has an important role to play in *educating* people, including adults, about the risks that they run when they smoke, drink, eat fatty foods, spend most of their leisure hours sprawled in front of television, and so on, but it should none the less not *prevent* them doing these things. As Mill put it, 'the inconvenience is one which society can afford to bear, for the sake of the greater good of human freedom'.

Mill's defence of liberty against the state involved demarcating a sphere of private activity within which people should have complete freedom to do as they liked. We have examined some problems with this approach, and we will encounter some more in Chapter 6 when we look at feminist arguments against the idea of a protected private sphere. So now I want to explore a different way of restricting what the state may do in the name of individual freedom.

10. John Stuart Mill, utilitarian, feminist, and defender of liberty.

This is the idea that every person has a set of *human rights* that governments must never infringe.

The idea of human rights has grown steadily in influence since the United Nations endorsed, in 1948, the Universal Declaration of Human Rights, which set out a long list of rights that all the signatory states undertook to respect in the case of their own citizens. But the concept itself can be traced back much further, to the idea of natural rights that played a central role in the earlier stages of liberal political philosophy. John Locke, for instance, claimed that all *men* at least (whether his exclusion of women was deliberate is controversial) had natural rights to life, liberty, and property, and when governments were established by social contract, they undertook to protect these rights as a condition of their having political authority. The Universal Declaration's list of rights is much more extensive, and besides rights that directly protect liberty – such as rights to freedom of movement, freedom of worship, and freedom to marry – it includes others whose effect is to provide people with access to material benefits, such as the right to work, the right to an adequate standard of living, and the right to education. Nevertheless, in the light of our analysis of freedom earlier in the chapter, these rights too can be seen as ways of protecting individuals' freedom, by ensuring that options are available to them that might otherwise be closed off by lack of material resources.

The human rights perspective does not involve asking whether certain human activities are potentially harmful to *others*. Instead it looks at the person herself and asks whether we can identify certain conditions without which no one can lead a decent human life. It tries to be neutral over the question what the best kind of life is for human beings – it does not say whether it is more valuable to be a religious believer, a political activist, an artist, a farmer, or a housewife – but it claims that all of these ways of living require conditions that human rights protect. Some of these conditions are plainly uncontroversial: no one can live a decent life without the freedom to think, communicate, and move about, without having adequate food and shelter, without having the chance to form personal and professional relationships with other people, and so forth. But other items that appear on standard lists of human rights, including the original UN Declaration, are more problematic. They may be rights that we would like to see implemented in the societies we belong to, especially if we are liberals, but we might wonder whether they are really essential to human life in all its forms.

Let us consider a couple of examples: first, the right to freedom of 'thought, conscience and religion', which the UN Declaration interprets broadly to include the freedom to change one's religion and the freedom to practise any religion in public or in private. Since religious belief and practice are pervasive features of human existence, we may agree that everyone should have the opportunity to worship, to read religious texts, and so forth. But should they be able to choose which religion to practise without restriction? Should they be able to proselytize (to try to convert people who adhere to a different religion)? Must the state treat all religions equally or is it permitted to privilege one as the national religion? In liberal societies the right we are considering is often interpreted strongly, as requiring a positive answer to all these questions. Yet elsewhere a much more limited right is recognized, and it would be hard to prove that human life in those societies is therefore less than decent.

Second, the UN Declaration includes a strong right of political participation. Everyone, it says, has a right to take part in the government of his country, and it goes on to say that this entails regular elections, universal and equal suffrage, and the secret ballot or its equivalent. Once again this is a right that liberals will applaud, and as we saw in the last chapter there are good reasons for wanting those who wield power to be democratically accountable to the people as a whole. But if we are talking about human rights, the question we must ask is whether such a right is really an essential component of a decent human life. For millennia human societies have existed in the absence of such democratic rights, and although by our standards all of them were imperfect, it would be hard to claim that they uniformly failed to provide tolerable conditions of life for their members.

In other words, we need to divide human rights, as they are conventionally understood, into two categories. There is a fairly short list of rights that we can say with some confidence are essential for human beings to possess, no matter how in particular they choose to live their lives. Deprived of these rights, their lives will be cramped, stunted, less than fully human. There is also a longer list of rights that we believe every citizen is entitled to enjoy, and that lay down parameters for a well-governed society. However, there may be different versions of this longer list, depending on who is compiling it. The version favoured by liberal societies may be different from the one preferred by societies with different cultural backgrounds, for example Islamic societies, or East Asian societies with Confucian or Buddhist traditions. So we might conclude that those rights that appear only on one of the longer lists and not on the shorter list should not strictly speaking be called human rights. When the French revolutionaries framed their statement of principle in 1789 they called it *The Declaration of the Rights of Man and of the Citizen*. Taking our cue from them, we might call the rights that belong on the longer list rights of citizenship, meaning by that that these rights ought to be recognized as basic protections for the individual *within our political community* – while in other communities a different set of rights, overlapping with but not identical with ours, should prevail.

I began this chapter by pointing out that the idea of an area of individual freedom into which government must in no circumstances intrude has become deeply ingrained in liberal societies. What we have discovered is that this idea is actually quite problematic. Once we began to investigate what freedom really means, we saw that in many cases it cannot be enjoyed without positive action on the part of government, providing the resources that keep options open, and the conditions under which people can make free and informed choices. We also found that there was no simple way of defining a sphere of 'self-regarding' activity which was of no concern to anyone beyond the individual inside it. And finally we have found that using human rights as a way of setting absolute standards for governments to observe can only work if the list of human rights is kept short and basic. The longer list of citizenship rights will legitimately vary from society to society, and that means that it is a proper subject for political debate. Rights that at one time seemed essential may later prove to be socially harmful (the Founding Fathers of America wanted to ensure that a citizen militia could always be raised to defend the country, and so the Second Amendment to the Constitution gives every American citizen the right to bear arms – a right that now prevents legislators from introducing any effective measures to control the spread of handguns).

Freedom, then, is a very important political value, but not of such importance that it should set absolute limits to the exercise of political authority. In a democracy, especially, questions about the use of resources to promote freedom, about freedom and social responsibility, and about the rights that all citizens should enjoy, will be openly debated, and in answering them people will appeal to many different principles – to equality, to fairness, to the common good, to respect for nature, to the protection of culture, and so forth. As these debates proceed, certain freedoms will be picked out and enshrined as basic rights, perhaps in a written constitution. But this is never the final word: as societies change, as new needs and new problems arise, so too will the shape of freedom itself. Who could have imagined, even 20 years ago, that internet access, electronic surveillance, or gene ownership would very soon assume centre stage in debates about individual liberty? Who can predict which new issues will have taken their place in 20 years' time?

Chapter 5
Justice

Lorenzetti's *Allegory of Good and Bad Government* has no place for the figure of Liberty, for reasons that we saw in the previous chapter, but Justice appears not just once but twice. She is one of the virtuous figures ranged alongside the good ruler, but she also appears separately, at the very heart of the fresco, a majestic figure seated alone between the two groups of figures representing good and bad government respectively. Why did Lorenzetti paint Justice twice? I think he wanted to convey the idea that justice is more than simply a virtue that rulers should possess: it is fundamental to the institutions that turn a mass of individuals into a political community in the first place. Lorenzetti's main figure holds a pair of scales, and from each of these a rope descends to the figure of Concord, who braids them into a thicker cord that then passes round the long line of citizens and up to the hand of the ruler. Justice, Lorenzetti is implying, binds the citizens one to another, and then all of them together to government. In this, he was following in a long-standing tradition which viewed justice as central to the justification of political authority. As St Augustine had asked, nearly a millennium earlier, 'justice removed, then, what are kingdoms but great bands of robbers?'

Saying that justice is of cardinal importance to good government is one thing; saying what justice really means is quite another, and this is the question that will occupy us throughout this chapter. One

11. Justice from *The Allegory of Good and Bad Government* by Ambrogio Lorenzetti.

thing we can be certain of is that the answer will not be simple. Lorenzetti's figure tells us that. One scale holds an angel representing Distributive Justice, and she is simultaneously severing the head of an evil-doer with a sword and placing a crown on the head of a meritorious recipient. The other scale supports Commutative Justice, and she appears to be conducting an exchange between two tradesmen, presumably ensuring that the metalworker's spear and the weaver's bale of cloth are of equal value.

Justice, then, has something to do with punishment and reward, and something to do with equality, but how should we define it? A very old definition, offered by the Roman Emperor Justinian, states that 'justice is the constant and perpetual will to render to each his due'. Taken by itself, this may not seem very informative, but it does at least point us in the right direction. First, it emphasizes that justice is a matter of each individual person being treated in the right way; it is not a matter of whether society in general is prosperous or poor, culturally rich or culturally barren, and so forth. This is not to say that the idea of justice for *groups* can be dismissed out of hand – and we shall be looking at it more closely in the following chapter – but the primary concern of justice is with how individuals are treated. Second, the 'constant and perpetual will' part of the definition reminds us that a central aspect of justice is that people must be treated in a non-arbitrary way: there must be consistency in how one person is treated over time, and there must also be consistency *between* people, so that if my friend and I have the same qualities, or have behaved in the same way, we should receive the same benefits, or the same punishment, depending on the circumstances.

The fact that justice requires consistency in treatment explains why acting justly is so often a matter of following *rules* or applying *laws*, since these guarantee consistency by laying down what is to be done in specified circumstances. But consistency alone is not enough for justice, as we can see if we imagine a rule that required all red-haired people to be put to death, or all those whose names begin with a 'D' to be paid at twice the normal rate. What these examples bring out is that justice requires *relevance*; if people are going to be treated differently from one another, it must be on grounds that are relevant to the treatment in question. This also implies that where there are no relevant grounds on which to discriminate, justice requires equality: everyone should be treated in the same way. How far equal treatment is required in practice remains to be seen, but we now have a second element of justice to set beside simple consistency: justice demands that people should be treated equally unless there are relevant reasons for treating them differently.

We can also add a third core element: the idea of proportion. This tells us that when people are treated differently for relevant reasons, the treatment they receive should be proportionate to whatever they have done, or whatever feature they have, that justifies the inequality. Many people believe, for instance, that if people work hard at their jobs that is a relevant reason for paying them more. But, for justice, there must also be proportionality: if Smith works twice as productively as Jones, he should be paid twice as much as Jones, but not ten times as much.

We have squeezed a fair amount of information about justice out of Justinian's formula, but we have not yet been able to say exactly what it is that people are owed as a matter of justice, nor on what grounds, if any, we are justified in treating them differently. And in fact there are no easy answers to these questions. This is partly because people frequently disagree with each other about what justice requires, in concrete terms, but also because the answer that anyone will give will depend to a great extent on who is doing the treating, what treatment is being given, and in what circumstances. To a very large extent, our ideas of justice are *contextual*, meaning that before we can decide whether a rule or a decision is fair we have to know a good deal about the situation in which it is being applied. Let me illustrate.

Suppose that I have been given £100 to allocate between five people who are now standing in front of me asking for their share of the money. What does justice tell me to do? So far, very little: it tells me that I should treat them consistently, that if I treat them differently this should be for relevant reasons, and that my allocations should be proportionate. Now let us fill in the context in different ways and see what allocations suggest themselves. The five people might be my employees, and the £100 might be the bonus they have earned this week, in which case I should consider how much each has contributed to our joint enterprise and reward them proportionately. Alternatively I might be an aid worker who has been given cash to distribute to allow starving people to buy food, in which case I should try to estimate what the relative needs of the five are and give more to those in greater need. Or again, the £100 might be the prize that has been offered for an essay competition, in which case what justice requires is that I should give it all to the person who has submitted the best piece. Or perhaps the £100 is a small lottery win, and the five people and I are members of a syndicate, in which case, clearly, we should share the sum equally between us.

Most readers, I imagine, will find my proposals about how the sum of money should be allocated in different circumstances more or less self-evident, and what this shows is that, although doing justice is a complex business, we already have a good intuitive grasp of what it involves in practice. Justice is less like a measuring rod than a box of tools: faced with a task – a decision to be reached or a rule to be applied – we know in most cases which tool to pull out and use. What is harder is to express this knowledge in the form of general principles – to create a *theory* of justice. But, as political philosophers, we need to develop a theory, because there are going to be cases in which our intuitions conflict, or perhaps run out altogether. This is particularly the case when we have to think about what *social* justice involves – justice not simply between individuals, but across a whole society. I shall explore this controversial idea later in the chapter. But first we need to explore the general principles of justice that we apply even in simple cases like the one above.

Notice to begin with that justice very often has to do not only with the treatment that people receive but with the procedure that is followed in order to arrive at that outcome. We can see this by thinking about criminal justice. It matters, of course, that guilty people are punished in proportion to their crime and that innocent people go free – that is what a just outcome requires – but it is also important that proper procedures are followed in arriving at a verdict, for instance that both sides are allowed to state their case, that the judge has no vested interest that would make him lean in one direction or the other, and so on. These procedures are important partly because they tend to ensure that the right verdicts are reached, but over and above that they matter because they show a proper respect for the people who are standing trial, who want to have the chance to state their case, to have the same rules applied to them as to other defendants, and so on. Imagine an arbitrary judge who decides each case by consulting tea-leaves, and suppose one day he happens to get all the verdicts right: has justice been done? The defendants would not think so (indeed studies have shown that in such circumstances people care more strongly about having fair procedures applied to them than about the actual outcome of their case) and nor should we.

In some cases, justice is *entirely* a matter of the procedure that is used to reach a decision – there is no independent standard that we can apply to the outcome. For instance if there is a nasty or dangerous job that needs to be done, and no reason why anyone in particular should do it (such as having special skills), we may draw straws to pick someone, and this is a fair procedure because everyone stands an equal chance of being chosen. Or a team may have to choose a captain, and decide this by voting – again a fair procedure because everyone's preference is counted equally. Occasionally procedures such as these have been used to decide bigger issues – for instance, random methods have been used to decide who is to be drafted into the army, or to select people to hold political office – but generally we are reluctant to understand justice in purely procedural terms. We want procedures that produce outcomes that are not merely random but are fair in a more substantial sense.

So what principles do we apply to decide when outcomes are fair? In the light of what was said earlier about the core concept of justice, an obvious candidate is equality – everyone should get the same amount of whatever it is we are allocating. This was the principle we applied in the case of the lottery win, and it applies more generally where there is some benefit to be distributed, or some cost to be borne, and there is nothing relevant that enables us to distinguish between the possible recipients. In these circumstances, there are two reasons favouring equality: the first is simply that any other way of allocating the benefit or the cost is bound to be arbitrary, in the absence of relevant reasons to discriminate, and the other is that we are likely to do more good all round by sharing both benefits and costs equally. Going back to our original case, suppose I know nothing at all about the five people claiming the £100, and I have to decide between giving it all to one person picked at random, and sharing it equally among the five. Procedurally either decision is a fair one, but the second outcome is likely to be better because, other things being equal, the first £20 is worth more to someone than additional increments. Suppose for instance that it turns out that the five people are starving: then if I give one person the whole £100, the other four may die. Of course there are circumstances in which the opposite holds – where you need £100 to stay alive, and £20 is useless. If I knew that, I should pick one person at random, since this at least gives each person a one in five chance of surviving. But cases like that are the exceptions. In general it is better to share benefits equally, and the same applies to costs – by spreading them as widely as possible, we make it less likely that anyone will suffer badly.

One principle of just distribution, therefore, is equality, and some political philosophers have claimed that it is the *only* principle – all justice is a kind of equality. But I believe this confuses the formal principle contained in the very definition of justice – that people should be treated equally unless there are relevant differences between them – with the substantive principle that everyone should actually receive the same amount of benefit or the same amount of cost. Because very often there *are* relevant differences between people. This is quite clear in the case of punishment, for example: no one has ever thought that everyone, innocent or guilty, parking offender or serial killer, should receive the same amount of punishment regardless. And the same applies when benefits are being allocated.

One good reason for not treating people in the same way is that they have different *needs*. No one objects to hungry or sick people being given more resources than people who are well-fed and healthy, at least so long as they have not created their own needs by behaving irresponsibly. However not everyone agrees that this is demanded by justice. There is a long tradition that holds that helping the needy is a matter of charity, which means it is something that people should be encouraged, but not required, to do. Lorenzetti would almost certainly have taken this view. Neither of his Justice figures shows any inclination to give handouts to the poor. That job is reserved for Magnanimity, who sits with a tray of gold coins on her lap to be dispensed when needy people appear. But as the state has come to assume responsibilities that were previously reserved for smaller communities – religious communities, artisans' guilds, and the like – so need has become a major element in the idea of social justice. The state is expected to ensure that each citizen has an income sufficient to cover basic needs for food and clothing, access to adequate medical care, and so forth.

But is it possible to distinguish genuine needs from other demands that people may make in the name of justice? Some critics think of needs as a kind of black hole into which all of a society's resources are likely to disappear if we say that justice requires us to meet them. So what does it mean to be in need? It means to lack something essential, where what is essential is determined partly by the standards of the society to which you belong. Some needs are universal, because they involve bodily capacities that are vitally important to human beings everywhere – people need to take in so many calories per day to be adequately nourished, they need access to clean water if they are not to contract diseases, and so on. But other needs are more variable because they depend on what is expected in the society someone inhabits. Everyone needs to be adequately clothed, but what counts as adequate clothing will vary from place to place. Everyone needs to be mobile – to have the capacity to move from place to place – but the extent of mobility, and the form it takes, will likewise vary. Needs, then, are the set of requirements that must be fulfilled if someone is to live a decent life in the society to which she belongs. They are socially relative, to some degree, but they are not merely subjective, as the critics claim. In economically developed societies, it is quite feasible to meet every citizen's genuine needs and still have ample resources to devote to other purposes – indeed there are sufficient resources in these societies to meet (locally defined) needs everywhere, if the political will existed to do so.

If unequal need is a relevant reason for departing from equality in one direction, unequal desert or merit takes us away from equality in a different direction. Again we must ask, what does it mean to deserve something? It means to have acted in a way that calls for a particular mode of treatment as a response to what you have done. A person deserves favourable treatment – a reward, an income, a prize, etc. – for acting in a way that others regard as admirable in some way, for instance contributing time and effort to a project that brings benefit to others; she deserves unfavourable treatment – blame or punishment – when her actions are deplorable, for instance involve harming other people. The basis on which you deserve varies from case to case, so we cannot say anything more specific about what someone has to do to become deserving. It is worth, however, underlining the link between desert and responsibility. What we deserve must depend on actions or performances for which we are responsible, so someone can escape punishment, for example, by showing that he was not responsible for the behaviour that caused the harm – say if he was being forced to act as he did, or if he was deranged. Equally, on the positive side, we cannot claim credit for the results of our actions that we did not intend and could not have anticipated. If I save a stranger's life, I deserve some reward – heartfelt thanks, at least – but if I rudely push him out of my way as I hurry along the street, and as it happens cause an assassin's bullet to miss, I deserve nothing of the sort. Saving his life was no part of my intention, and so I cannot claim responsibility for it.

Desert plays a central role in most people's understanding of justice, but like the need principle it has also come under attack from various quarters. Critics often claim that it can too easily be used to justify large inequalities in income and wealth, and it is certainly true that highly paid people are eager to claim that their contribution to society is such that their salaries are no more than a fitting reward for what they have done. Perhaps, though, this is less a problem with the idea of desert itself than a problem of finding an accurate way of measuring the size of contributions. A more philosophical objection holds that people are never really responsible for their behaviour in the strong sense needed to justify claims about desert. Look behind a person's performance and you find a train of causes that stretches back beyond the person herself. She was born with certain capacities and certain propensities, including propensities to choose to behave in one way rather than another, and had others instilled in her by her family, so any 'credit' for good behaviour or 'blame' for bad behaviour should really be directed to her genes and her parents. This objection to desert raises fundamental questions about personal responsibility that I cannot tackle here, but I think it is worth noticing what a radical step it would be to dispense with the idea altogether. If we were entirely to stop praising and blaming, rewarding and punishing, other people, our social interaction would change in a very basic way – indeed we would hardly be treating them as *people* at all. Once we recognize this, we can see that the real issue is not whether desert should play any part in the way we understand justice, but how large a part it should play. In particular, how far should it be allowed to govern the distribution of material resources like income and wealth?

Need and desert give us two very basic reasons why justice can require us to treat people differently. There are other reasons too, of a less basic kind. For instance people often form legitimate expectations about how they are going to be treated which may have nothing to do with either need or desert, and sometimes justice demands that we should honour these expectations. Promising and contracting are obvious instances of this. Reverting to my original example, it may be the case that I have promised £100 to one of the five people now standing before me, in which case that may be a good enough reason to give him the whole sum. Another set of reasons that may justify special treatment include restitution or compensation. Someone who has unjustly been deprived of a benefit to which they were entitled has a claim to have that benefit restored to them, or failing that, to be compensated by being given something else of equivalent value. (I describe these reasons as less basic because they presuppose that the expectations have been formed in a context that is already substantially just.) Once again we see that doing justice is a complex matter, that what counts as giving someone his or her due is to a large extent contextually determined.

So far I have been looking at justice in general terms, and not specifically at the role played by governments in promoting it. In the remainder of the chapter I want to explore the idea of *social* justice – the idea that we can put in place a set of social and political institutions that will ensure the just distribution of benefits and costs throughout society. This idea first emerged in the late 19th century, and stood at the heart of political debate throughout the 20th. It requires the state to become much more closely involved in distributive issues than was possible for states in earlier periods, even if their members had wished it. It is also a controversial idea: whereas only a few extreme sceptics have attacked the idea of justice as such, social justice has been pilloried, mainly by critics from the libertarian right, who see it as corrosive of personal freedom, and especially of the economic freedom that a market economy requires.

Let us look a little more closely at the attack on social justice. Critics such as the Austrian economist-cum-philosopher Friedrich Hayek argued that there was a fundamental error involved even in talking about social justice in the first place. According to Hayek, justice is fundamentally a property of individual actions: an action is unjust when it violates a general rule that a society has put in place to allow its members to cooperate with one another – so, for instance, theft is unjust because it violates a rule protecting property. But if we look at how resources – money, property, employment opportunities, and so forth – are distributed across a society, we cannot describe this distribution as either just or unjust, since it results not from the actions or decisions of a single agent, but from the actions and decisions of millions of separate people, none of whom intended to create this or any other distributive outcome in particular.

Hayek is certainly right to point out that 'social distribution' cannot be attributed to any single distributing agency, given the complexity of any society in the contemporary world. But what he overlooks is that the distributive pattern that we observe around us does, in its general outline, depend upon the institutions we have created, consciously or unconsciously – for instance the prevailing rules governing property and contracts, the system of taxation, the level of public expenditure on health care, education, and housing, employment policies, and so on. These are all institutions that can be changed by political decision, and so if we leave things as they are that is equivalent to a decision to accept the existing distribution of resources. Moreover we can understand, again in general outline if not in precise detail, what the effect of a proposed institutional change would be. To that extent, the distribution of resources across society – who gets which benefits, how wide the spread of incomes will be, etc. – is something that, in a democracy, is under our collective control. It is a perfectly reasonable, therefore, to ask what a fair distribution of social resources would look like – to ask what social justice would require us to do.

This is not to say, however, that social justice is something that we ought to pursue. Hayek's second claim is that, in attempting to make the distribution of resources match up to our favoured principle of distributive justice, we would destroy economic freedom and thereby kill the goose that lays the golden eggs. Let us assume Hayek is right when he claims that a market economy is the most effective way of organizing production and exchange, and that any alternative would involve an intolerable reduction in living standards in economically developed societies. The question is whether pursuing social justice means turning your back on the market economy, or whether it is possible to pursue that aim *through* a market economy, albeit one that has been shaped in the right way, and has other institutions working alongside it.

Here we need to look at different ways of interpreting the idea of social justice. The most radical version, embraced by Marxists and some of the communitarian anarchists we encountered in Chapter 2, reduces social justice to the principles of equality and need. A just society, on this view, is one in which each member contributes to the best of his or her ability, but resources are distributed according to need, with any surplus being shared equally. There is no room here for the idea that people need incentives, or deserve material rewards for making their contribution. Could such a society exist? On a small scale it undoubtedly could. We have many examples of communities whose members practised social justice in this radical form among themselves. Most of these communities had a religious basis, and depended on religious authority to sustain the ethos whereby each member worked for the common good of the community without expecting any personal reward, but there are also instances – most notably the kibbutzim in Israel – of secular communities achieving the same goal. These communities dispensed with the market, at least internally. They relied on what are sometimes called 'moral incentives' – people contributing either because they simply believe that they should, or because they feel the eyes of their neighbours upon them.

The question is whether a large society could practise social justice in this form. It seems that the informal coordination of people's behaviour that can occur in a small community cannot happen here – the economy must either be market-based, giving people incentives to produce the resources that other people want to consume, or state-directed, with a central authority planning what is to be produced and directing individuals according to the plan. Although in theory one can imagine both market and centrally planned economies that do not rely on material incentives, in practice this has proved impossible to achieve (attempts were made in the mid-20th century by Communist regimes in China and Cuba to replace material by moral incentives, but in neither case was the experiment successful). Pursuing social justice in its radical form does seem to require dispensing with the market and reconstructing society on a quite different, communitarian basis.

There is, however, a less radical view of social justice which has been embraced by many democratic socialists, and also by many contemporary liberals. On this view, social justice requires the equal distribution of some social benefits – especially equal rights of citizenship such as voting and freedom of speech. It requires some benefits to be distributed on the basis of need, so that everyone is guaranteed an adequate income, access to housing and health care, and so forth. But it also allows other resources to be distributed unequally, so long as there is equal opportunity for people to try to acquire a larger share. These inequalities may be justified on grounds of desert, or on the grounds that by giving people material incentives to work hard and produce goods and services that other people want, everyone in society benefits.

12. John Rawls, author of the hugely influential *A Theory of Justice*.

Perhaps the most influential interpretation of social justice of this kind is the one developed by John Rawls, who in his book *A Theory of Justice* argued that a just society must fulfil three conditions. First, it must give each member the most extensive set of basic liberties (including political liberties like the right to vote) that is consistent with the same liberty for everyone else. Second, social positions carrying greater advantages – higher paying jobs, for instance – must be open to everyone on the basis of equality of opportunity. Third, inequalities of income and wealth are justified when they can be shown to work to the benefit of the least advantaged members of society – in other words when they provide incentives that raise the society's overall productivity, and therefore allow more resources to be channelled to those at the bottom of the heap.

Rawls's theory of social justice explicitly makes room for a market economy: his third principle is formulated so as to allow for the possibility that people may need to keep at least part of the gain that they can make through producing goods and services for the market if they are going to be sufficiently motivated to work hard and use their talents in the most productive way. This undermines Hayek's claim that social justice and market freedom are conflicting goals. On the other hand, a market economy governed by Rawlsian principles would look quite different from the economic systems that exist in most liberal democracies today.

To begin with, Rawls's idea of equality of opportunity is quite radical. It is not enough that positions of advantage should be given to those who, at the moment of selection, can be shown to be better qualified to hold them. It must also be true that applicants have had an equal opportunity to become qualified, which means that, from the moment of birth on, people of equal talent and equal motivation should have been given the same chances, in school and elsewhere. Clearly this condition is very far from being realized in any existing society. Furthermore, Rawls's third principle, usually called 'the difference principle', permits inequalities only when they can be shown to benefit the worst off. In practice this would mean that governments should set tax rates so that benefits were continually redistributed from rich to poor, up to the point at which the productivity of the better off begins to decline and the tax yield therefore decreases. Although most democratic states have tax regimes that are somewhat redistributive, they all fall far short of this requirement. Taxes are set in such a way that an adequate level of welfare services is provided for all citizens, but no government attempts, as a former Labour Chancellor, Denis Healey, was reported to have proposed, to 'squeeze the rich until the pips squeak'.

My own view is that a theory of social justice should retain Rawls's first two principles – equal liberty and equality of opportunity – but replace the difference principle with two others. The first is that of a guaranteed social minimum, understood in terms of the set of needs that must be met to give every citizen a decent life; as I indicated earlier, this minimum is not fixed, but changes between societies and over time. The second is a principle of desert: inequalities of income and wealth should be proportional to the relative contributions different people make, measured by their success in producing goods and services that other people need and want. Like Rawls's theory, these principles do not entail getting rid of the market economy, but they do require the state to maintain an extensive welfare system, and to adjust the legal framework within which the market functions so that there is as close a link as possible between what people contribute economically and what they receive by way of income. This would require some big changes to the way that capitalist economies currently operate, since existing rules of property ownership and inheritance allow people to reap large rewards by virtue of luck, inherited wealth, corporate position, and so forth – factors that are unrelated to their contribution to society. Indeed the pursuit of social justice may point us towards a form of market socialism in which economic enterprises are owned and controlled by those who work in them, rather than by outside shareholders, so that profits can be shared among the actual producers. This is not the communist utopia favoured by Marx and other radical socialists, since it allows harder working and more talented individuals to reap the fruits of their labour, but it still takes us far beyond the political agenda of the present day, at least so far as the liberal democracies are concerned.

Like democracy, social justice is an unfinished project. The political philosopher's job is to tell us, in outline, what a just society would look like, without either building castles in the air, or over-adapting to the political realities of the moment. Many now believe that the quest for social justice has been stalled by global developments which reduce the power of any state to regulate the market economy as justice demands. I shall return to this question in the final chapter of the book. But first I want to turn to a different challenge to justice as it has traditionally been understood – the challenge posed by feminists and multiculturalists.

Chapter 6
Feminism and multiculturalism

In Western democracies today, debates about the position of women and minority cultural groups command a great deal of political attention. Feminists and multiculturalists often claim that the issues that concern them – issues about the nature of personal identity, about whether it is possible to draw a line between public and private life, about respect for cultural difference – have displaced the questions about authority, democracy, freedom, and justice that I have been examining in previous chapters. Indeed, the very nature of politics itself has changed: it now has less to do with what happens in the institutions of government, and more to do with what happens between individuals – men and women, whites and blacks, Christians and Muslims – in their everyday interactions. Political philosophy, therefore, needs to be rewritten with an entirely new focus.

I believe such claims are exaggerated, and in this chapter I shall try to explain why. The issues raised by feminists and multiculturalists are certainly very important, and should shift the way we think about politics. But they should not displace the older questions, which remain as urgent as they ever were. Instead they give these questions a new dimension. My aim here is to explore how far feminist and multiculturalist arguments should make us think differently about political authority, democracy, freedom and its limits, and justice.

One way to keep perspective is to ask about the circumstances under which feminism and multiculturalism have moved to the centre of political debate. Or, to turn the question round, why was it that for many centuries the relations between men and women, and the position of minority cultural groups, were routinely ignored in treatises of political thought? It is tempting to see this either as some kind of gigantic oversight, or else to argue that dominant groups in society kept such issues off the agenda. It is certainly true, to take the case of feminism, that political philosophy in the past was written by men who took it for granted that the subordination of women to men was a natural fact, that women had no active part to play in political life, and so on (there were occasional exceptions – John Stuart Mill was one – but these were few and far between). But they took it for granted mainly because nobody was arguing the opposite case. Although with hindsight we can take them to task for their chauvinism – and many books have been written in this vein – it is both more useful and in a way more honest to ask what it is about own society that makes us take feminist and multiculturalist arguments so seriously. How can we see things that our predecessors so notoriously failed to see – for instance, that there is absolutely no reason why women should not enjoy the same set of career opportunities as men?

The answer, I believe, is that we live in societies that are founded on commitments to freedom and equality, but that have failed so far to live up to these commitments in the case of women and people from minority cultures. It is one of our deepest beliefs that each person should be able to live life in the way that he or she chooses, subject to certain limits that we explored in Chapter 4; it is another deep belief that each person is entitled to be treated as an equal, either by being given equal rights, or by being given equal opportunities. Given these beliefs, it becomes a matter of great political concern if one section of society enjoys only a smaller area of personal freedom, or receives less than equal treatment at the hands of existing social and political institutions. So, for instance, when women are denied the option available to men of harmoniously combining a career with family life, or when members of ethnic minorities have fewer opportunities in the job market than others, this means that they are not being treated as fully free and equal members of their society. It is tempting sometimes to complain that feminists, especially, are arguing on behalf of the already privileged. We read about a woman employed in a top city institution bringing a court case because her share options are worth so many millions less than those of her male colleagues, and we think that by any reasonable comparative standards she is already doing extremely well. This reaction is right in one way but wrong in another. It ignores the experience of being discriminated against in a society that is committed to equal treatment, which entails being devalued as a person despite one's comfortable lifestyle.

Feminists argue for ways of transforming society so that women enjoy full, not merely nominal or partial, freedom and equality. Multiculturalists advance similar claims on the part of ethnic, religious, and other groups whose members are discriminated against or whose culture is undervalued by the dominant majority. Each position comes in different versions, but rather than trawl mechanically through these I want to explore the general challenge that feminism and multiculturalism pose to the ideas laid out in earlier chapters.

Let us begin with the issue of political power and political authority. In Chapter 2 I treated this as a question about the authority of the *state* – in other words I assumed that at least in modern societies when we ask about the form that political authority should take, we are asking about how the state should be constituted. But many feminists have challenged this way of understanding politics. They have argued that it is problematic, if not impossible, to draw a line between the public sphere, where people engage in political relationships with one another, and the private sphere, where relationships are non-political. In other words they see politics as a much more pervasive phenomenon, one that touches every aspect of our lives. This challenge is summed up in the slogan 'the personal is political'. And it follows that if we are going to talk about political authority, we have to talk not only about the authority wielded by states over their subjects, but also about the authority wielded by men over women.

What gives bite to this challenge is the undoubted fact that men, not only in the past but also to some extent today, have exercised power over women. They have done so partly by keeping them economically dependent – in order to survive women have had to rely on male breadwinners – partly by promulgating ideas about women's proper role in life that women themselves have come to accept, and partly by sheer physical force – the threat of violence if male commands are disobeyed. These are general claims about relations between the sexes, and it is not being suggested that every individual man has used all three means to keep women in check – for one thing women have often found ways to fight back – but they do none the less point to a kind of power that has usually remained invisible in political philosophy. When political philosophers like Hobbes write about power struggles and how to control them, they are thinking about relationships between men – it is as though the issue of relations between the sexes had already been resolved.

However, it does not necessarily follow that we should now begin thinking of these relations as political. Although politics is about power – about who should have it, how it should be controlled – not every power relationship is a political one. Take some familiar examples – the power of a teacher over his pupils, the power of an employer over her workers, the power of a general over his soldiers. In each case the first party can get the second party to behave in ways that he or she wants, partly through exercising authority that is voluntarily accepted, partly through being able to threaten certain consequences – detention, the sack, a court martial – if instructions are not obeyed. So why are these relationships not political ones? We need to think about what makes politics a distinctive part of human life. First, although it involves making and enforcing decisions, it involves making them in a certain way –

13. The price of women's liberation: the suffragette Emmeline
Pankhurst arrested outside Buckingham Palace, 1914.

giving different voices and different interests a chance to make themselves heard. It is not necessarily democratic – there can be politics in royal courts – and it is not necessarily morally pure – threats and bargaining come into it, as well as discussion and argument. But where a dictator can impose his will without needing to listen to any other voices or consult interested parties, there is no politics. Second, political authority potentially touches upon every aspect of human life. Although we can and should set limits to it – we ought to mark out spheres of personal freedom where political decisions cease to intrude, as we saw in Chapter 4 – the very act of marking out these spheres is a political act. And politics is also the means whereby we determine what powers individual people in different walks of life should be able to wield. It is a matter for political decision how far a teacher's authority over her pupils should extend, what the respective rights and obligations of employers and workers should be, what generals should and should not be allowed to do in the course of managing an army.

If politics has these distinctive features, then we can put the feminist challenge to political authority in a different form. What feminists are pointing out about relationships between men and women is not so much their inherently political nature as the *failure of politics* to address them. Political authority, in the form in which it has been constituted up to now, has not set adequate parameters for the peculiarly intimate relations that exist between the sexes. It has failed in a number of ways: it has not given women adequate physical security, especially protection against domestic violence, it has not ensured that women enjoy equal rights with men in a number of important areas of life, and it has not provided women with sufficient personal freedom (I shall be looking in a moment at what this means). It is these political failures that have allowed men to exercise power over women in their personal lives, and one obvious reason is that women have for centuries been almost entirely excluded from politics in the conventional sense.

This leads us directly to the feminist and multiculturalist critiques of democracy as it is currently practised, but before examining those I want to look more closely at the issue of freedom. As we saw in Chapter 4, freedom is usually understood in terms of a protected sphere of action in which each person has the opportunity and means to decide how to live his or her own life. Feminists – and similar arguments have been voiced by multiculturalists – have challenged this idea in two ways. First, they have argued that women are in reality much less free in the private sphere than political philosophers usually assume. Second, they have argued that behaviour that might appear to be purely 'self-regarding', to use Mill's phrase, can in fact have damaging effects on women's interests.

Freedom, we saw, involves having a range of options open to one, but also having the capacity to choose between them. In the past, the options open to the great majority of women were clearly very limited. They had little choice but to marry, rear children, and work either within the household or in a limited number of occupations closely connected to it. The 20th century saw a dramatic change in this external aspect of women's freedom. Not only were almost all occupations at least formally opened up to women, but there were now genuine choices to be made in the sphere of personal relations – whether to marry, whether to engage in heterosexual relationships at all, whether to have children, and so forth. This is not to say that they enjoyed *equal* freedom with men in all these respects, because freedom, as again we saw, is also a matter of the costs that are attached to different courses of action, and very often women had to bear extra costs when, for example, they decided to combine a career with raising children. The harder issue, however, has to do with the internal aspect of freedom – the capacity to choose.

Feminists have argued that women remain in thrall to long-established cultural norms in their society even where they are no longer physically compelled to conform to them. These norms have to do especially with how women should look, how they should behave, what kind of relationship they should establish with men, and so on. These norms become embedded in a woman's psyche at an early stage in life, and are very difficult to challenge later on. Women obviously do make real choices in many areas of life – in occupation, religion, lifestyle in a broad sense – but nearly always within bounds set by prevailing ideas of femininity. And this may lead to damaging outcomes – for instance an obsession with physical appearance may lead to anorexia among teenage girls, beliefs about the domestic roles of men and women may lead women to submit to a monstrously unfair division of domestic chores, and so forth.

What makes this issue so hard to tackle is that it becomes entangled with another question that feminists themselves disagree about: whether men and women have essentially a common nature, or whether there are deep differences between them which mean that there will always be contrasts in the way that men and women prefer to lead their lives. If the latter is true, then we should not be too quick to assume that when women choose to follow certain cultural norms, these choices are inauthentic. This does not mean that we have to accept the norms that lead teenage girls to starve themselves, for instance. But it is at least possible that it is ingrained in women's nature to be more concerned about their physical appearance than men, in which case it is not detrimental to their freedom that the choices they make in this part of life display a different pattern from the choices made by men.

How can we decide whether observed male–female differences in choice are merely the result of cultural norms that could be changed, or whether they reflect differences that are hard-wired into the sexes? This is such a complex issue that the wisest course may be to follow John Stuart Mill and remain agnostic. As Mill wrote in *The Subjection of Women* (one of the very few examples of feminist political philosophy before the 20th century):

I deny that anyone knows, or can know, the nature of the two sexes, as long as they have only been seen in their present relation to one another. If men had ever been found in society without women, or women without men, or if there had been a society of men and women in which the women were not under the control of the men, something might have been positively known about the mental and moral differences which may be inherent in the nature of each.

Since we lack this evidence, we have good reason to ensure that the external conditions of freedom are the same for men and women – that the options they have available to them, and the costs they will incur if they take them up, are the same. Whether beyond this we must also try to break the hold of prevailing cultural norms about how men and women, respectively, should behave, or whether instead we should try to ensure that traditionally female norms are valued as highly as traditionally male norms – this, as I say, remains a matter of intense dispute among feminists themselves.

Cultural minorities – groups whose religious or ethnic identity is different from that of the majority in their society – also face barriers to personal freedom. Even though, in modern liberal societies, they have the same formal set of educational and career opportunities as members of the majority, there are often special costs attached to pursuing these options. For instance, jobs may be specified in such a way that people from minority groups have difficulty in complying with the specifications – there may be dress requirements that conflict with religious or traditional dress codes, the working week may be organized in such a way as to be incompatible with religious practices, say if people are required to work on the day that is prescribed as the Sabbath, and so on. Multiculturalists argue that opportunities must be made equal in a more than formal sense. The problem here is that the costs themselves may appear to be matters of choice. If, for religious reasons, I choose not to eat pork, say, then clearly that is not a limitation on my freedom: the restriction is self-imposed. So how is it different if, because I insist on wearing a certain style of dress, many employers won't offer me a job? I could choose not to dress in that way.

To tackle this problem, we need to decide whether a dress code, or indeed any other type of job specification, is one that is essential to the job we are considering. In some instances, dress requirements may be imposed for safety reasons. In other cases aesthetic questions may be involved – actors and dancers, for instance, have to be prepared to wear the gear that the production designer has chosen. But if the code is not much more than conventional, then cultural minorities can claim with justification that unless it is abandoned or relaxed their freedom of occupational choice has been limited. (Of course they must also demonstrate that their own dress requirement has deep cultural roots, so that breaching it would be costly for the individuals in question.)

We see, then, how feminist and multiculturalist challenges may force us to revise, not the idea of freedom itself, but our understanding of the conditions under which people are genuinely free to choose their path in life. The same applies when we look at the limits of that freedom. In Chapter 4 I gave examples of how behaviour that might appear to be merely offensive to other people, and therefore not 'other-regarding' according to Mill's definition, might become more than that if the people affected by it were forced to change their own behaviour as a result. Feminists and multiculturalists may want to push this argument further. They would claim, for example, that the way women and cultural minorities are portrayed, especially in the popular media, can have major repercussions for the way they are treated generally. If women are represented as sex objects, for instance, or blacks are portrayed as criminals or drug-dealers, then this will affect, perhaps unconsciously, the behaviour of people who are hiring for jobs, or deciding promotions. The implication is that freedom of expression should be more limited than we had previously thought. Expression that is damaging to the interests of vulnerable groups should be prevented. Some feminists have for this reason called for pornography to be banned; representatives of religious minorities have argued for blasphemy laws that prohibit derogatory statements about their religions, as some Muslims did after Salman Rushdie published his book *The Satanic Verses*.

These claims pose problems for societies that are strongly committed to individual freedom. After all isn't freedom valuable precisely because it allows people to challenge conventions, to shock and outrage, and in that way get other people to question their existing beliefs? How can we salute expression or behaviour that offends one group of people, and then turn round and try to ban expression or behaviour that offends another group? Because the line between forms of expression that are liberating despite being offensive to some and forms of expression that are merely offensive is difficult to draw, we may conclude that the law is a blunt instrument in this area – that in general people should be left to judge for themselves which expression is acceptable and which is not, with exceptions only for extreme cases, such as racist speech in public places. This does not exclude public debate about these issues, which can make people more aware about what others with different cultural backgrounds find offensive or insulting. In a multicultural society widespread respect for the cultural values of other groups is an important good. At the same time it is important not to succumb to debilitating political correctness. Where cultures contain elements that are hostile to freedom and equality – especially freedom and equality for women – we should not hesitate to say so forcefully, even if this means giving offence.

I now turn to the question of democracy. In societies with universal suffrage, a major issue for both feminists and multiculturalists has been the relative absence of women and representatives of cultural minorities from legislative assemblies. Why should this matter? It is argued on the other side that representatives are elected by all of their constituents, and are answerable to them, so even if there are few women and minority members actually present, their interests and concerns will still be channelled through the (white) men who

14. Muslims burn *The Satanic Verses* in Bradford, UK, 1989.

represent them. It is mechanisms of accountability that matter, in other words, not who actually gets chosen to sit in Parliament or Congress.

This reply overlooks the fact that, in democracies as they presently exist, elected representatives have a great deal of freedom to decide issues on which their constituents have never been given the chance to pronounce. In Chapter 3 I discussed ways of deepening democracy, of involving the people more fully in the making of decisions, and if that were to happen it might indeed matter less who was chosen to represent them. But now it matters a good deal, and the argument for increasing women's and minority representation is that there are important issues on which it is very hard for those who do not belong to these groups to understand fully the perspectives and interests of those who do. So, for example, if a question about religious practice comes to Parliament or Congress, say in relation to a case of job discrimination, it is important that there should be people present who can explain the meaning of the practice, its centrality or otherwise to the life of the group in question, and so on. The same applies when an issue of specific concern to women arises, for instance an issue about maternity leave or childcare.

It is not essential that representation should be strictly proportional to numbers in the population. What is important is that each significant perspective be adequately represented in the legislative body. This follows from my earlier description of democracy as a system of reaching political decisions by open discussion among all those involved. Here it is assumed that the people involved are willing to listen to arguments on the other side, weigh them using standards of fairness, and change their own views accordingly. Of course democracies do not always work like this, but for minority groups especially it is important that they should, as far as possible. They are, after all, minorities. If everyone just votes according to their sectional interest, the minorities are bound to lose. The force of argument is their only weapon.

This view has been challenged by some feminists and multiculturalists, who claim that the very idea of deciding issues by reasoned argument biases the system in favour of those who are already adept at discussion of this kind. They argue that women and minority groups may need to make use of more impassioned forms of speech to make their case; they also suggest that certain issues should be reserved for the groups that have the greatest stake in them, so that questions about reproductive rights – abortion, contraception, etc. – should be left for women alone to decide. In Chapter 3 I argued in relation to the general problem of minorities that democracies ought to be willing to enshrine certain basic rights in a constitution, precisely so as to protect minorities against unfriendly majorities at any moment. I also suggested that creating separate constituencies to deal with different issues, as happens in a federal system, could be justified on democratic grounds. However, the problem here is that many of the issues that deeply concern women and cultural minorities are also of considerable concern to other groups. Abortion is an obvious case. However tempted one might be to think that this is a matter of concern only to women, it is plain that religious groups, in particular, are also deeply concerned, believing as they do that abortion involves the destruction of a human being with a soul. One cannot dismiss this concern as simply crazy, unless one is willing in the same way to dismiss all other cultural claims with a religious basis. So the only way forward is to attempt to work out, through debate and discussion, a position on abortion that is at least minimally acceptable to the opposing sides, and this again underlines the importance of having a full range of perspectives represented in the body that has to reach a decision.

Finally in this chapter, we come to the question of justice: how have feminists and multiculturalists challenged prevailing ideas of social justice, and how ought we to respond to these challenges? I want to focus here on two particular issues: domestic justice – justice between men and women in family life – and positive discrimination – measures designed to favour women and ethnic minorities in access to higher education and the job market.

Social justice, as I indicated in the last chapter, concerns the way in which social and political institutions produce a distribution of benefits and costs among individuals. The focus has traditionally been on the system of property and taxation, on the public provision of health care and education, and so forth. But can we restrict our attention to the distributive effects of these public institutions? Feminists argue that we also need to look at what happens inside the family unit, to see how *that* distributes benefits and costs, and also to see what impact it has on the wider distribution of jobs, income, and so forth. More specifically they argue that, without domestic justice, social justice is never going to be achieved for women.

Many people today would agree that historically the family gave women a raw deal – that it placed them more or less at the mercy of their men folk, who not only expected to do very little work in the home, but also controlled the family finances by virtue of their status as breadwinners. But it might seem that now that women have won their independence in the public sphere – have gained legal rights, political rights, and equal access to the labour market – relations between men and women in domestic contexts must also have changed profoundly: they now interact on terms of equality. In other words, once social justice (in the familiar sense) is achieved for women, domestic justice will follow. But this optimistic belief has not been borne out in practice: women's position has undoubtedly improved in many respects, but there is still a great deal of inequality, especially in the way domestic labour is shared between men and women. Even when both partners work full time, women still carry out the lion's share of household tasks. On the assumption that these tasks are burdensome (does anybody actually enjoy vacuuming or ironing?), this looks unfair.

Women are also disadvantaged by the fact that, when children are born, they almost invariably take longer career breaks than men, often coming back into the job market to take up part-time work, or in any case advancing up the promotion ladder less rapidly than their male counterparts. This, as much as overt sexual discrimination, seems to explain the often-observed fact that women systematically earn less than men, and are poorly represented at the top of the various professions (there are very few women chief executives, judges, professors, etc.).

But we should not be too quick to conclude that because men and women end up unequally placed in certain respects, this must be an injustice. After all some unequal outcomes are none the less fair – for instance when they reflect the different choices people have made. So one response that we need to consider to the evidence I have just presented is that women have agreed to the arrangements that appear to work to their disadvantage – that they have accepted as part of the family deal, so to speak, that they should do most of the housework, and that they should have less glittering careers than their male partners.

Why might they have agreed to this? Presumably because there still exist norms about the respective roles of men and women, norms which tell us that women have a special responsibility for home-making and child-rearing, while men have a special responsibility to earn income outside the home. So although in practice the vast majority of women of working age are employed in the labour market, there is a tendency for both sexes to regard their work as a kind of bonus, something added on to their primary responsibilities. But even if women share in this perspective, it is clearly one that works against them in terms of the balance of costs and benefits. The norm is a relic from an earlier age, and its being freely embraced is not sufficient to make it fair (even slaves have been known to accept norms that justify their slavery).

Showing that domestic justice has not been achieved in our society is one thing; saying more positively what fairness within the household requires is harder. Should we insist that equal sharing of costs and benefits must be the rule for all couples, or is there room for people to work out different arrangements according to their circumstances? Perhaps once the old norms about a woman's proper place have disappeared, the principle of free agreement will come into its own. As we saw, some feminists insist that there are deep differences between men and women, especially is connection with their role in child-rearing, and see strict equality as forcing women to behave in ways that deny their maternal natures. To the extent this is true, fairness in domestic relations ought to be compatible with flexibility in family life, where partners can choose to divide up work inside and outside the home according to their individual preferences and abilities.

Finally in this chapter we need to look at the issues raised by affirmative action and positive discrimination policies. Both feminists and multiculturalists have challenged conventional ideas about equality of opportunity, which imply that when people are being selected for jobs or college places, this must be strictly on the grounds of merit. Instead, they argue, justice may require us to discriminate positively in favour of women and/or members of ethnic minorities – in other words selection committees should build in a weighting factor that takes account of whether an applicant belongs to one of these categories. Such policies have of course been implemented quite widely, both by universities and by employers, but they remain controversial.

We need to distinguish two justifications that might be given for positive discrimination policies. One is that standard ways of measuring 'merit' – for instance relying on examination grades or test results – tend to underestimate the true ability of women or minority members. This might be because the tests contain hidden cultural biases, or because people in these categories have had fewer opportunities to acquire the skills that the tests are designed to measure – as a result, say, of having a weaker educational background. Where this can be demonstrated – it is much more plausible in the case of deprived ethnic groups than in the case of women, given that girls now tend to outperform boys at school – positive discrimination policies are actually a better way of achieving equal opportunity. There is no dispute at the level of principle: the argument is simply about the best way to ensure that those who are selected for advantaged positions are the people who really deserve them.

However, there is a second justification that *does* raise issues of principle. This starts from the fact that women and ethnic minorities are currently very significantly underrepresented in the higher echelons of society, and presents positive discrimination as the best means to put this right. In other words, it should be an important aim of social policy to ensure that there are many women, blacks, Muslims, and so forth, holding high-level positions in business, the professions, the civil service, and so forth. From this perspective, social justice is not simply about the fair treatment of individuals; it also has an important group-based element. A just society would be one in which all major groups were represented in the various social spheres in rough proportion to their numbers.

Suppose it were true that individual opportunities were genuinely equal – that people were always chosen for jobs and other positions on the basis of merit, and had the same chance to develop the skills and abilities that count as merit – but nevertheless different groups in society turned out to be more or less successful overall, some occupying most of the top posts, others clustering at the bottom. Could we say that the less successful groups were the victims of group injustice? Not if their members had consciously chosen not to apply for the better jobs, say for cultural reasons. But this seems unlikely in general (there might be specific jobs that groups find uncongenial for cultural reasons). A more likely explanation is that groups whose members historically have tended to occupy low-status jobs have low expectations and a diminished sense of self-esteem, and therefore few of their members believe that they have any chance of climbing high up the career ladder – so they prefer not to try.

15. **Multicultural harmony: the Notting Hill Carnival, 1980.**

This state of affairs should concern us. It is bad both for the groups in question and indeed for the whole society that their status is low and that individual members do not seize the opportunities that they might have taken. Positive discrimination policies may help, by showing what minority members are capable of once they are given an initial boost – say a place at a good university. Such people can act as role models encouraging others to follow their lead. So perhaps such policies can be justified, on balance, in terms of their overall effects (African-Americans probably provide the best example). But this does not mean that they are required as a matter of justice, or that groups with low aspirations and low levels of achievement can be described as victims of injustice on that count alone. Indeed there may be a real conflict of values here – between treating individuals fairly, and ensuring that ethnic and other groups are fully integrated into the life of the wider society. I said near the beginning of the book that political philosophers ought to resist the temptation, common to politicians, to assume that the policy they favour involves no sacrifice of other values. Here we ought to conclude that positive discrimination is just only when it is a matter of ensuring real fairness between individuals – unearthing genuine merit. If it goes beyond that, and becomes a means of raising the general standing of one group in relation to others, then however desirable that may be in general, it is no longer a matter of justice.

I suggested at the beginning of the chapter that we should not see feminism and multiculturalism as displacing longer standing questions of political philosophy, but as posing these questions in new ways. I hope now to have justified that remark. Feminists and multiculturalists teach us to think differently about political authority, freedom, democracy, and justice, and in particular challenge us to say how these values are to be realized in societies that are culturally diverse and in which women expect to be treated as the equals of men. Their writings enrich political philosophy and bring it directly into contact with some of the most hotly debated issues of the present day.

Chapter 7
Nations, states, and global justice

In the last chapter, we explored some basic questions about the *scope* both of political authority and of justice. We asked what made some human relationships political, and others not, and we asked whether the idea of justice could be applied to relationships between men and women in the domestic sphere, and to relationships between different cultural groups within a society. This chapter will also be about the scope of politics and justice, but now we will be looking outwards rather than inwards. We will be asking whether the political units we are most familiar with – nation-states – have now outlived their usefulness, and whether we ought to be thinking of politics as something that takes place on an international or even global scale. And we will also examine what justice might mean at a level beyond the nation-state: can we think in terms of global justice, and if so are the principles that apply at this level fundamentally different from the ones that apply within national political communities?

These questions about scope and scale are not just technical. The way human beings interact with one another changes quite fundamentally as we move up from small face-to-face groups where each person knows the others as individuals, to large societies where our knowledge of most other people is of a general kind – we know them only as types, or categories – and we gain our knowledge indirectly, through reports in the media, for instance. It is worth backtracking a little to look at how the city of Siena functioned in the days of Lorenzetti, our mural painter. By comparison with the political units that dominate the world today – nation-states – its scope was tiny. Beyond the city proper, Siena had jurisdiction over an area not more than 30 miles in radius from its centre, covering small towns, villages, and countryside. The total population of this political unit has been estimated to have reached a maximum of about 100,000 people before the Black Death struck in 1348; of these about half lived in the city itself, and only a minority of residents qualified for citizenship. So Lorenzetti, whose *Allegory of Good and Bad Government* has many features that identify it with Siena, was portraying a political community whose political leaders would be known personally to many of the citizens, and who would be seen from day to day going about their business within the city walls. The General Council, made up of representatives from each part of the city, was summoned by a town crier and by the ringing of a bell. When we describe this as a political *community*, we mean exactly what we say.

Political philosophy as we understand it today first arose in these small-scale political communities – most notably in classical Athens. Here the body of citizens was in control of its own destiny, at least as far as the internal life of the city went, so there was a great deal of point in asking questions about the best form of government, about the qualities that good rulers should posses, about the meaning of justice, and so forth. Perhaps city-states of this kind provided human beings with the best opportunity they have ever had to govern themselves well – to achieve freedom, justice, and democracy. So why have they not survived? The answer is that city-states like Athens and Siena were always vulnerable to being captured and absorbed by larger units; they had constantly to be willing to fight to preserve their independence, and to do this they had to form shaky alliances with neighbouring cities, which might succeed for a time, but in the longer term proved incapable of resisting more centralized empires: Athens succumbed to Philip of Macedonia, while Siena, after preserving a modicum of independence by putting itself under the protection of nearby rulers such as the duke of Milan, was finally conquered by the Spanish Emperor Charles V. City-states did not fail because of their internal deficiencies, but because of their external weakness in the face of invading armies.

The political unit that proved capable of resisting imperial power while still embodying some of the virtues of the city-state was the nation-state. This was formed on a much larger scale, involving millions of people occupying a large geographical area, with the institutions of the state itself – the parliament, court, government, military command, etc. – concentrated in the capital city, but it could still make some claim to be a political community because its members thought of themselves as belonging to a distinct people or nation, separate from their neighbours. For this to happen, there had to be media of communication that brought the many localities that made up the nation-state into contact with one another, telling the people in each what the others were thinking and doing. The historian Benedict Anderson has for this reason called nations 'imagined communities': unlike face-to-face communities, their very existence depends on a collective act of imagination. People had to learn to see themselves as French, or American, or Japanese, not just as family members or residents of a particular town.

But do nations really exist? Or are they not just imagined but entirely imaginary? Is there anything that genuinely differentiates the people who live on one side of a national boundary from their counterparts on the other side? Dean Inge once said that 'a nation is a society united by a delusion about its ancestry and by a common hatred of its neighbours'. Like most good quotations, this one contains more than a grain of truth. National identities very often do emerge out of antagonism towards some neighbouring people: being British was once very much a matter of not being French, as today being Scottish is a matter of not being English, and being Canadian a matter of not being American. Nations also typically develop myths about themselves – about their unique moral or cultural qualities, about their past military or political (or sporting) achievements, and so forth. None the less national identity is not simply illusory and it serves good purposes as well as bad. The groups we call nations share, in nearly all cases, a common language, a history of living together over time, and cultural traits that are expressed not only in literary form but also in the physical environment – in the way towns and cities are built, in the pattern of the landscape, in monuments, religious buildings, and the like. When new generations are brought up in those cultural and physical surroundings, they cannot help being shaped by this common heritage – even if they rebel against many aspects of it.

The influence of national culture is particularly strong in the case of nations that have states of their own, because here cultural transmission takes places through the laws, the institutions of government, the education system, and the national media, as well as through the informal channels just mentioned. Nation and state reinforce one another – the power of the state is used to strengthen national identity, while people who are tied together in this way are more willing to accept a common political authority and rally to its

16. Canadians rally for national unity against Quebec separatism, Montreal 1995.

defence when it is attacked. This explains why nation-states have proved to be relatively successful as political units: they are large enough not to be engulfed by imperial armies, yet at the same time they can call upon the loyalty of their members when resistance is necessary.

There is, of course, a downside to this loyalty. When nation-states fight one another, as they did in the two world wars of the 20th century, they can inflict death and suffering on a scale that would have been unthinkable in earlier periods, where wars were most often fought primarily by mercenary armies in the service of empires. So to defend the nation-state as a political unit, it is not enough to highlight its military capacities. We need to say something more about what can be achieved politically in a society whose members are held together by a common identity.

Here I want to make two claims. The first is that such an identity makes democratic government very much more likely to work successfully. Looking back to what was said in Chapter 3, we saw that one of the great difficulties in democratic politics is to reconcile majorities and minorities – to persuade the minority group to accept the decision of the majority, while at the same time persuading the majority not to trample on the wishes or the interests of the minority but to try to accommodate them when reaching decisions. I suggested there that one of the factors likely to encourage what we might call 'democratic self-restraint' was trust between the parties. In a society where people are generally trusting of others, they are less anxious about finding themselves in a minority on some issue, more willing to allow the majority to implement its decision, on the basis that no very great harm will come to them. Where trust is absent, or evaporates, by contrast, every decision becomes potentially a life-and-death issue.

Consider a simple case: suppose that we have a democratic constitution, and the party we belong to has just been defeated in a general election. Should we hand over power as the constitution requires, or should we stage a coup and declare the election null and void? In handing over the reins of government we are exposing ourselves to risks of two sorts. The first is that our opponents will use their new-found power to persecute us, or at the very least introduce discriminatory measures designed to favour their own supporters. The second is that, despite having come to power through a democratic election, they will not respect the constitution, so that by handing power over now, we are forfeiting the chance of ever wielding it again. (This is not just a theoretical possibility. It is well known that, in the case of fledgling democracies, the key moment is not the first election, but the point at which the party that has won the first election is defeated and is required to give up office: what will it do?) Whether we are willing to take that risk depends on how much trust we have in the people who will now take office.

To complete the argument, we need to ask what makes people more likely to trust others, particular others who are not known to them personally. Social psychologists who have investigated this question have found that one important factor is perceived similarity: we are inclined to trust those who we believe resemble us in one way or another. It is not difficult to think of explanations for this: it may be a trait that we have inherited from the early stages of human evolution, when people cooperated with one another in extended kin groups, and had to learn how to discriminate between insiders and outsiders. In large-scale societies, where people may look and sound very different from one another, trust is a problem. But national identity can help to solve it: we may disagree politically with the other side, we may even despise much of what they stand for, but we know that they still have a good deal in common with us – a language, a history, a cultural background. So we can trust them at least to respect the rules and the spirit of democratic government.

My second claim is about social justice. What makes people willing to support policies that will promote social justice, particularly when they can see that they will stand to lose when these policies are implemented? For instance they may have to pay higher taxes to create the resources that are needed to provide adequate welfare services for all citizens, whereas it would be cheaper for them to purchase health care, education, and so forth privately. Or in order to create equal opportunities for groups that have hitherto lagged behind, they may have to relinquish some of their existing privileges, like giving their offspring fast-track access to jobs and college places. Why might they do this? From a sense of justice or fairness, we might answer. But again we need to ask: what makes people willing to deal with others on terms of justice, and to answer *this* question we need once again to consider the issue of shared identity.

It is true of course that we recognize some obligations of justice to people everywhere, regardless of whether we share anything with them beyond our common humanity. We know that it is wrong to kill, injure, or imprison them without good cause, and that if they are in danger or distress we should come to their aid. This common knowledge can help us make sense of the idea of global justice, as I shall later show. But social justice imposes much greater demands on us – in particular it often requires that we accept restrictions placed on us by principles of equality when we could do better for ourselves, or our friends and relations, by casting those restrictions off. No one is killed or injured if we cheat on our taxes or bend the rules to give a nephew a nice job he doesn't deserve. So what might motivate us to accept these demands? As political philosophers like John Rawls have emphasized, one very important motive is the wish to live together with people on terms that we can all justify to one another. In other words, if somebody asks me to explain my behaviour – explain why what I am doing is acceptable – I can do so by appealing to principles that she and I can both accept.

The strength of this motive will depend on how closely tied we are to the other people involved – it is most powerful in small face-to-face groups – but national communities provide at least some of the cement that makes people concerned to live with others on terms of justice. I am not claiming that within existing nations people always conduct themselves justly – that is far from being the case – but only that they have a motive to do so, and this makes them more willing to support policies involving progressive taxation or equal opportunity legislation of the kind I mentioned earlier.

People who disagree with these claims linking national identity to democracy and social justice often point by way of example to countries such as Belgium, Canada, and Switzerland, which are multinational – they each contain two or more distinct national communities – and yet are stable democracies that support extensive welfare states and other institutions of social justice. In reply, I want to say two things. First, these states have evolved federal systems that devolve many important decisions, including decisions about economic and social policy, to provinces or regions that encompass different national groups. In Belgium, for example, Flemings and Walloons have separate governments responsible for many areas of policy such as employment and housing, alongside the federal government which deals with Belgium-wide issues such as defence and foreign policy. Second, most people in these societies have what we might call 'nested' national identities: they think of themselves *both* as Flemish and as Belgian, as Quebecois and as Canadian, and so forth. In other words, they share in an inclusive national identity as well as in a more localized one, and this helps to explain why these societies work as effectively as they do – they can call on common loyalties to support democratic institutions at national level and to justify redistributing resources from their richer regions to their poorer ones.

Nation-states, then, have allowed people to work together politically on a large scale, achieving democracy and pursuing social justice with at least partial success, through the creation of common political identities that can bind people together despite their conflicting beliefs and interests, and their geographical dispersal. But many now believe that this form of government has become outmoded. Countless obituaries for the nation-state have already been penned, and we are just waiting, it seems, for the body to topple conveniently into the grave.

Why is the nation-state thought to be obsolescent? Some of the reasons are internal, having to do with the difficulty of sustaining common national identities in societies that, through immigration and for other reasons, are becoming increasingly multicultural in character. Other reasons concern the external environment in which states now have to operate: their diminished capacity to control global economic forces, and the widening range of problems – especially environmental problems – that can only be solved by cooperation between states or by international bodies. I do not intend to add anything to the existing flood of literature on these topics, but instead ask some questions about the kind of political order that might take the place of the nation-state.

The most favoured alternative is some form of cosmopolitanism. Cosmopolitanism is in fact a very old idea, dating back to the Roman Stoics, who liked to think of themselves as *kosmopolitai*, 'citizens of the world'. But what exactly does this mean? One interpretation of cosmopolitanism is world government in a literal sense – the replacement of the 191 separate states that now exist by a unitary political authority. But although world government has been advocated by some, its disadvantages are only too evident.

First, it is very hard to envisage how government on this scale could possibly be democratic. It would clearly have to work through elected representatives, each representing millions of people, and so ordinary citizens would have virtually no opportunity to influence or control the government itself. The thrust of my argument in this chapter is that democracy works best on a small scale: the city-state was probably its ideal site, and the nation-state's great achievement has been to simulate the intimacy of the city by its use of the mass media, giving people at least a sense that they are involved in, and able to influence, political affairs. But world government would appear a distant and alien body, as even, on a much smaller scale, the European Union does to many people today. And the issue of trust, highlighted earlier, would emerge with all its force: why would I regard as legitimate decisions taken by a majority drawn from communities with which I feel myself to have little in common?

Second, there is a real risk that a world government might become tyrannical, and if that were to happen there would be no sanctuary in which individuals could take refuge. In a world of states, a clear sign of bad government is a government that has to build walls and fences to keep its people captive, and where alternatives exist the walls and fences cannot be kept up indefinitely (the Berlin Wall, built to prevent the people of East Germany escaping to the West, lasted for 28 years before it was torn down block by block in 1989). Despotic governments are kept in check, at least to some degree, by the possibility of people escaping to places where they can live in greater freedom and security. But there would be no such check if world government became a reality.

Finally, if increasing cultural diversity is currently posing problems for many nation-states, the problems would be far deeper for a world government that had to embrace the major civilizations that exist today, each of which would aim to see its values and beliefs reflected in public policy. Indeed there are only two circumstances in which such a proposal would seem at all feasible. One would be the emergence of a common global culture that engulfed present-day cultural differences, presumably one based on mass-market consumerism – the so-called 'McWorld' scenario, where everywhere turns into a kind of giant American shopping mall. The other would be a wholesale privatization of culture, so that although different groups in different places pursued their own cultural values, there would be no expectation that government should take these cultural values into account (think, by way of analogy, of a society in which there are no state churches, only churches built and funded by their own congregations). This is perhaps more plausible (and less offputting) than the first scenario. Yet one of the fiercest divisions in

17. Resisting globalization, US-style: Latvia 1996.

today's world is between those who are willing to see culture (and especially religion) privatized in this way, and those who insist that government policy should be based on their preferred cultural values.

World government in the literal sense must be distinguished from the much more modest proposal, favoured by among others the philosopher Immanuel Kant, that states should enter into a permanent agreement with one another to renounce the use of force; there should be a confederation to ensure what Kant called 'perpetual peace'. We can see this foreshadowed in the relations between liberal democracies today, which involve a sometimes tacit and sometimes explicit agreement to settle their differences by negotiation or by reference to international bodies such as the European Union or the United Nations. Agreements of this kind, it is important to emphasize, stabilize relations between states, but leave states themselves as the main sources of political authority. And Kant himself favoured this: a single world government, he thought, would be a 'universal despotism which saps all man's energies and ends in the graveyard of freedom'.

Cosmopolitanism in its most literal sense is both implausible and unattractive. But political philosophers sometimes interpret the idea of world citizenship differently, not as a form of government, but as a proposal about how individuals should think and behave. What is being suggested is that we should overcome our narrow national and other attachments and think of ourselves as if we were citizens of the world, in other words as people who have equal responsibilities to our fellow human beings everywhere. From this perspective, national boundaries are simply arbitrary dividing lines to which no moral significance should be attached. In particular we should cease to think of justice as something to be pursued primarily within the limits of the city or the nation; we should give equal weight to the claims of every human being, regardless of race, creed, or nationality. So even if political authority remains localized in particular nation-states, we should use it to promote global justice, ceasing to give any preference to those who fall inside the political community we happen to belong to.

Cosmopolitans of this stripe often do not deny what was said above about the relationship between our communal identities and our willingness to accept obligations of justice to other people. They may agree that very often people's sense of justice is powerfully shaped by their sense of belonging, by the division between those inside and those outside our political community. But they see this as a problem to be overcome, not as a permanent limitation. There are deep issues involved here, about the extent to which human beings are capable of acting on principles of reason alone, or on the other hand whether reason has to be allied to feelings and emotions, our sense of who we are, in order to motivate behaviour. But rather than grapple with these, I want to signal a couple of reasons for doubting at least strong versions of ethical cosmopolitanism, and then propose an alternative way of understanding global justice.

One of these reasons assumes that we will continue to live in a culturally divided world – in other words that the 'McWorld' scenario I referred to earlier does not come to pass. Culture affects the way that we understand justice, not perhaps at the most basic level, but certainly in terms of the kind of demands that can properly be seen as demands of justice. Religion furnishes some obvious examples. Suppose someone claims that he has special needs because of his religious beliefs, or that his opportunities are being limited by religious practices that he is required to comply with. How should we regard his claims? If we stand within the religious tradition to which he belongs, and we accept his interpretation of that tradition, then we will see his claims as valid claims of justice. But if we look in from the outside, we are bound to regard them differently. We might see the claims as having some weight, but we are also likely to ask whether the tradition could not be changed so that it becomes less onerous for the faithful.

A similar difference of perspective may occur at international level. Suppose I belong to a predominantly secular society, and am committed to cosmopolitan principles of justice that require me to disregard national boundaries. A second society is materially much poorer than mine, but this is largely because its members devote a large fraction of their resources to a priestly establishment, claiming that they have no option but to do so – God has commanded it. How strong a claim on my resources does a person in that society have? Should I regard his relative poverty as something he has chosen, for religious reasons, and therefore as making no special demands on me, or should I regard the religious expenditure as externally compelled, and therefore consider his needs as more pressing than those of people in my own society? The general point is that if cultural differences have an impact on the way that we understand justice, then what justice requires *across* a culturally plural world becomes indeterminate.

A second reason has to do with the connection between justice and reciprocity. The basic idea is simple to state: I behave justly towards other people in the expectation that they will behave justly towards me in return. This does not mean that what I do and what they do will be exactly the same. Our circumstances may be different. But if, say, I help somebody who is now in need – suppose I come across somebody who is stranded late at night because she has missed the last bus home – I do so on the assumption that were I in that position, she or someone else would do the same for me. Within political communities, this idea of reciprocity is given concrete shape through the legal system and other forms of government. When I obey traffic regulations or pay my taxes, I assume that my fellow-citizens will also comply, either voluntarily or in order to avoid legal sanctions. Without this assurance, behaving justly opens you up to being taken advantage of by those with fewer scruples.

If we apply this thought to cosmopolitan justice, the problem is obvious. Assuming that I know what justice requires me to do for someone who belongs to a distant community, what reason do I have to expect him to reciprocate? How do I know that my willingness to act justly is not going to be exploited? Of course this does not *prevent* me from doing what justice requires, but it does make it a more costly option. This problem might be avoided if there were to emerge shared global norms whereby people everywhere recognized certain situations as making demands of justice upon them – these have been foreshadowed in a very limited way in the case of large-scale natural disasters, where it has now become the norm to organize an international relief effort to bring help to the victims. So we might move slowly into a world in which certain forms of just behaviour would be reciprocated. But until that happens, someone setting out to act on cosmopolitan principles of justice – in the sense of principles that take no account of national boundaries or other forms of membership – is behaving heroically, doing more than she is morally required to do.

This does not mean that there is no justice beyond the boundaries of the nation-state. There *is* such a thing as global justice, and it is an increasingly important factor in world politics, but we should not understand it, as cosmopolitans do, as simply social justice stretched out beyond those boundaries to embrace people everywhere. I want to conclude this chapter, and the book, with a brief sketch of this non-cosmopolitan alternative. It has three main elements.

First, there is a set of conditions that define just terms of interaction *between* nation-states. Some of these are already familiar from handbooks of international law. States must abide by the treaties and other agreements they have made; they must respect one another's territorial integrity; they must not use force against another state except in self-defence; and so on. But there are other requirements that are less familiar, and have only recently come to play a part in the conduct of international relations. These requirements have to do with the way the costs and benefits of international cooperation are shared. There are, for instance, a number of environmental problems whose solution requires nation-states to place constraints on their citizens' behaviour. Quotas for the emission of greenhouse gases are one example; quotas for catching endangered species of fish are another. The problem is to decide how these costs should be distributed, and principles of justice can help to settle this (unfortunately the answer is often not clear-cut – different principles can reasonably be called into play – which inevitably leaves space for power politics to intrude).

There are also important issues concerning the terms of international trade. Rich and powerful countries are currently able to set these terms in such a way as to leave them free to export their products to less developed countries, while imposing barriers to protect their own farmers that make it difficult for producers in those countries to export their crops. There are arguments for, and arguments against, leaving international markets completely free, but what justice requires is that whatever restrictions are imposed on trade should be ones that give people in poor countries the same set of economic opportunities as their counterparts in rich countries.

Second, global justice involves respecting and protecting the human rights of people everywhere, including, if necessary, challenging the authority of states that violate these rights. I looked at the idea of human rights in some detail in Chapter 4, and I argued there that we need to draw a line between basic human rights – rights to those conditions that human beings everywhere need if they are to live minimally decent lives – and the longer lists of rights that appear in many human rights documents, which are better understood as rights that particular political communities should secure to their citizens. This distinction is important here, because from the perspective of global justice it is only protection of the basic rights that matters. We should not intervene in other states simply because they fail to recognize rights that *we* think are important, such as rights to universal suffrage or unlimited religious freedom (we may *encourage* such states to implement rights on the longer list by offering them inducements of various kinds – for instance membership in international bodies such as the European Union – but we should not to try to enforce them).

Why do human rights impose obligations of justice on us regardless of national or other cultural boundaries? On the one hand, they mark out genuinely universal features of human existence that transcend cultural differences. You and I may reasonably disagree about the importance of religious belief and practice, but we cannot reasonably disagree about whether someone who is being tortured or allowed to starve to death is being harmed. So the argument I presented earlier about why ideas of social justice are not cultural universals does not apply here. On the other hand, human rights carry great moral weight. They correspond to the most serious kinds of harm that can befall a person. So they override our concerns about fairness and reciprocity. This difference is something that we instinctively recognize. If someone who is not in serious need asks me for my help – let us say requests a lift down to the station – then I am likely to consider whether he is taking advantage of my good nature or whether he would be willing to do the same for me on another occasion. But if he has been seriously injured in an accident, all that matters is that I am in a position to help him. Protecting human rights corresponds to the second case. If they are not protected, people will suffer or die. So anyone who can help must do so as a matter of justice.

The third requirement of global justice is that people everywhere should have the opportunity to be politically autonomous; that all political communities should enjoy rights of self-determination. This does not mean that every nation must have its own independent state. In some cases people are intermingled geographically in such a way that this simple formula for self-determination cannot be applied. None the less, there are forms of self-determination that can be used in such cases, such as the power-sharing agreement between Protestants and Catholics in Northern Ireland that is proceeding in fits and starts as this book is

18. Universal human rights: actors Julie Christie and Cy Grant marking UN Human Rights Day.

being written. What can frustrate the search for self-government? Either the political ambitions of neighbouring states who want to impose a form of imperial rule on the community in question, or an economic position that is so precarious that the community is given no real choices to make. In either case, other nations have a responsibility to work together to create the conditions under which self-determination is possible.

Why is this a matter of justice? In my argument against political cosmopolitanism, I emphasized how important it is to many groups that they should be allowed to express their cultural traditions politically, and this can only be done if they enjoy political self-determination. Even liberal societies attach great value to national self-determination, and only relinquish their rights of sovereignty with great reluctance. This is evidence of the strong need people have to feel in control of their own destiny, even those who are not active participants in democratic government. If these observations are accurate, then being denied the opportunity for self-determination is a serious loss, one great enough to impose obligations of justice on others.

If global justice along these lines were achieved, the world would look something like this: political authority would rest primarily with nation-states, but they would collaborate to ensure that the costs and benefits of international cooperation were fairly distributed. Each political community would govern itself according to its own political traditions, and schemes of social justice would likewise vary somewhat from place to place. But everywhere human rights would be respected, and in cases where they were threatened, either by natural disasters such as drought or by oppressive regimes, other states would work together to ward off the threat. Some states would be richer than others: this would not be unjust provided that it resulted from political choices and cultural decisions rather than from economic exploitation. Some states would also be more democratic than others, but even those peoples who did not control their governors directly would identify with their government and feel that it represented their interests and values.

Such a world is very different from our own. It is what John Rawls in his book *The Law of Peoples* called a 'realistic utopia' – an ethical vision that stretches the bounds of political possibility as far as they can be stretched without becoming pure pie-in-the-sky. Are we likely to get there? Many current observers of the international scene foresee a kind of market triumphalism, in which global economic forces prevent any nation-state from making real political choices. Self-determination becomes meaningless if the only option is to adopt policies that ensure maximum economic competitiveness. But, as I said in Chapter 1, this form of fatalism looks no better grounded than previous forms that we now regard as antiquated. In any case, if there really are no political choices left for us to make, then political philosophy, whether national or international in focus, becomes useless, nothing more than fiddling while Rome burns. Everything I have said in this book assumes that the choice between good and bad government is always one we have to make, even if the form that good government takes changes as technology advances and societies become larger and more complex.

We have come a long way from the picture of good government in a city-state of 100,000 people. It is harder for us than it was for Lorenzetti to describe the conditions under which people can till the ground, trade, hunt, teach, and dance in relative peace and security – or on the other hand to describe how tyranny and oppression bring devastation and slaughter in their wake. Our politics is conducted on a much larger scale, and at many different levels. It is much more difficult to connect cause and effect, and therefore to assign responsibility for political success or failure. Yet there are elements in Lorenzetti's picture that are as relevant to us now as they were in 14th-century Siena: the difference between legitimate political authority and tyranny; the relationship between government and its citizens; the nature of justice. These questions remain at the heart of political philosophy, and it is at precisely those moments when we feel that humanity's future is slipping out of our control that we need to think about them long and hard, and then decide, together, what to do.

Further reading

General reading

For readers who want to explore the topics covered in this book in greater depth, several textbooks on political philosophy can be recommended:

Jonathan Wolff, *An Introduction to Political Philosophy* (Oxford University Press, 1996).

Adam Swift, *Political Philosophy: A Beginners' Guide for Students and Politicians* (Polity Press, 2001).

Will Kymlicka, *Contemporary Political Philosophy*, 2nd edn. (Oxford University Press, 2002).

Dudley Knowles, *Political Philosophy* (Routledge, 2001).

Gerald Gaus, *Political Concepts and Political Theories* (Westview Press, 2000).

Robert Goodin and Philip Pettit, *A Companion to Contemporary Political Philosophy* (Blackwell, 1993).

The history of political philosophy poses greater problems. Perhaps because of the huge weight of historical scholarship that has accumulated, academics today are deterred from writing single-author overviews of the subject. Two introductory multi-author books are David Muschamp (ed.), *Political Thinkers* (Macmillan, 1986) and Brian Redhead (ed.), *Political Thought from Plato to Nato* (Penguin, 1995); these treat individual political philosophers in historical sequence. Two studies which use historical figures to illustrate general themes in political philosophy are Jonathan Wolff's book referred to above and John Morrow, *History of Political Thought* (Macmillan 1998). For an in-depth treatment of political thought from Hobbes onwards, see Iain Hampsher-Monk, *A History of Modern Political Thought* (Blackwell, 1992). For short accounts of both major and minor figures in the history of political thought, see my *Blackwell Encyclopaedia of Political Thought*, co-edited with Janet Coleman, William Connolly, and Alan Ryan (Blackwell, 1987).

Chapter 1

Lorenzetti's frescos are reproduced and discussed in Randolph Starn, *Ambrogio Lorenzetti: The Palazzo Pubblico, Siena* (Braziller, 1994). They can also be viewed on the internet at *http://www.kfki.hu/arthp/ html/l/lorenzet/ambrogio/governme/index.html*. In interpreting the frescos, I have been much helped by Quentin Skinner's essays on Lorenzetti, which are reproduced in his *Visions of Politics*, ii (Cambridge University Press, 2002).

Marx's theory that politics is largely determined by a society's form of material production can be found in *The Communist Manifesto* and the preface to *A Critique of Political Economy*, both of which are reproduced in standard selections from Marx such as *Karl Marx: Selected Writings*, ed. D. McLellan (Oxford University Press, 1977). The 'end of history' thesis was popularized in Francis Fukuyama, *The End of History and the Last Man* (Hamish Hamilton, 1992).

For Hobbes and Plato, see respectively Thomas Hobbes, *Leviathan*, ed. R. Tuck (Cambridge University Press, 1991) and Plato, *The Republic*, available in many translations including that of H. D. P. Lee (Penguin, 1955) – the simile of the cave can be found in book 7.

For the contrast between ancient and modern forms of democracy, see Sanford Lakoff, *Democracy: History, Theory, Practice* (Westview Press, 1996).

Chapter 2

The most accessible discussion of political authority that I know of is April Carter, *Authority and Democracy* (Routledge & Kegan Paul, 1979). More advanced is Leslie Green, *The Authority of the State* (Clarendon Press, 1998).

Hobbes's description of life without political authority is in his *Leviathan*, ed. Richard Tuck (Cambridge University Press, 1991), ch. 13; the passage cited occurs on p. 89. A good introduction to his thought is Richard Tuck, *Hobbes* (Oxford University Press, 1989).

I have discussed anarchism at greater length in *Anarchism* (Dent, 1984). The best known communitarian anarchist was the Russian Prince Peter Kropotkin – see for instance his *The Conquest of Bread and Other Writings*, ed. M. Shatz (Cambridge University Press, 1995). The most important work of libertarian political philosophy is Robert Nozick, *Anarchy, State and Utopia* (Blackwell, 1974), though note that Nozick ends up by defending the minimal state rather than anarchy. For a good discussion see Jonathan Wolff, *Robert Nozick* (Polity Press, 1991).

On public goods, and the question whether political authority is needed to provide them, see David Schmidtz, *The Limits of Government* (Westview Press, 1991).

The problem of political obligation is discussed by John Horton in *Political Obligation* (Macmillan, 1992). The most persuasive case for the fair-play argument is to be found in G. Klosko, *The Principle of Fairness and Political Obligation* (Rowman & Littlefield, 1992); it is criticized, along with the consent argument, in A. John Simmons, *Moral Principles and Political Obligations* (Princeton University Press, 1979).

The grounds for civil disobedience are discussed in Peter Singer, *Democracy and Disobedience* (Oxford University Press, 1973).

Chapter 3

John Locke's critique of Hobbes can be found in his *Two Treatises of Government*, ed. P. Laslett (Cambridge University Press, 1988). The quotation is from the *Second Treatise*, ch. 7, p. 328.

The Schumpeter quotation comes from Joseph Schumpeter, *Capitalism, Socialism and Democracy*, ed. T. Bottomore (Allen & Unwin, 1976), p. 262.

The Rousseau quotation comes from Jean-Jacques Rousseau, *The Social Contract*, ed. C. Frankel (Hafner, 1947), p. 85.

On democracy in general, see Ross Harrison, *Democracy* (Routledge, 1993) and Albert Weale, *Democracy* (Macmillan, 1999). For the pluralist approach, see Robert Dahl, *Democracy and its Critics* (Yale University Press, 1989). For a defence of popular participation in politics, see Benjamin Barber, *Strong Democracy* (University of California Press, 1984) and John Burnheim, *Is Democracy Possible?* (Polity Press, 1985).

For evidence about how ordinary citizens might perform if asked to make political decisions, see Anna Coote and Jo Lenaghan, *Citizens' Juries* (IPPR, 1997) and James Fishkin, *The Voice of the People* (Yale University Press, 1995).

On the role of constitutions, see Geoffrey Marshall, *Constitutional Theory* (Clarendon Press, 1971).

Chapter 4

John Stuart Mill's *On Liberty* is included in *Utilitarianism; On Liberty; Considerations on Representative Government*, ed. A. D. Lindsay (Dent, 1964). The quotations in this chapter are from pp. 125 and 138.

I have collected together what I regard as the best essays on the concept of liberty, including Isaiah Berlin's, in *Liberty* (Oxford University Press,

1991). Other good treatments are Tim Gray, *Freedom* (Macmillan, 1991) and Adam Swift, *Political Philosophy* (Polity Press, 2001), part 2.

Mill's principle of liberty has been much discussed. Recommended books include C. L. Ten, *Mill on Liberty* (Clarendon Press, 1980) and Joel Feinberg, *Harm to Others* (Oxford University Press, 1984).

For discussion of the issues of free speech raised by the controversy surrounding Salman Rushdie's *The Satanic Verses*, see Bhikhu Parekh (ed.), *Free Speech* (Commission for Racial Equality, 1990) and Bhikhu Parekh, *Rethinking Multiculturalism* (Macmillan, 2000), ch. 10.

The development of the idea of natural rights is traced in Richard Tuck, *Natural Rights Theories: Their Origins and Development* (Cambridge University Press, 1979). For analysis of the more recent idea of human rights, see James Nickel, *Making Sense of Human Rights* (University of California Press, 1987) and Henry Shue, *Basic Rights* (Princeton University Press, 1996).

Chapter 5

St Augustine's remark about justice comes from *The City of God against the Pagans*, ed. R. W. Dyson (Cambridge University Press, 1998), p. 139.

I have analysed the idea of justice at greater length in *Principles of Social Justice* (Harvard University Press, 1999) – this focuses on the principles of equality, desert, and need. A good discussion of different theories of justice can be found in Tom Campbell, *Justice*, 2nd edn. (Macmillan, 2001), as well as in the general textbooks by Kymlicka and Swift listed above. For the idea that different principles of justice apply in different contexts, see especially Michael Walzer, *Spheres of Justice: A Defence of Pluralism and Equality* (Basic Books, 1983).

A good selection of recent writing by political philosophers on equality is Matthew Clayton and Andrew Williams (eds.), *The Ideal of Equality* (Macmillan, 2000).

Hayek's critique of social justice can be found in Friedrich Hayek, *Law, Legislation and Liberty*, vol. ii. *The Mirage of Social Justice* (Routledge & Kegan Paul, 1976).

Evidence about communities and societies that have tried to dispense with material incentives is presented in Charles Erasmus, *In Search of the Common Good: Utopian Experiments Past and Future* (Free Press, 1977).

John Rawls's masterwork is *A Theory of Justice*, first published in 1971 (revised edn., Harvard University Press, 1999), but a shorter and more accessible version of his theory can be found in *Justice as Fairness: A Restatement*, ed. E Kelly (Harvard University Press, 2001).

For an accessible introduction to the idea of market socialism, see Julian Le Grand and Saul Estrin (eds.), *Market Socialism* (Clarendon Press, 1989).

Chapter 6

Both feminism and multiculturalism are discussed at length in Will Kymlicka, *Contemporary Political Philosophy*, 2nd edn. (Oxford University Press, 2002). There are many anthologies of feminist political thought, including Alison Jaggar and Iris Marion Young (eds.), *A Companion to Feminist Philosophy* (Blackwell, 1998) and Anne Phillips (ed.), *Feminism and Politics* (Oxford University Press, 1998). On multiculturalism, see Will Kymlicka, *Multicultural Citizenship* (Clarendon Press, 1995), Bhikhu Parekh, *Rethinking Multiculturalism* (Macmillan, 2000), and for a critique, Brian Barry, *Culture and Equality* (Polity Press, 2001).

For the claim that in debates about political power and authority, the power of men over women has remained unacknowledged, see especially Carole Pateman, *The Sexual Contract* (Polity Press, 1988). For analysis of how political philosophers have regarded women in the past, see Susan Okin, *Women in Western Political Thought* (Virago, 1980).

The quotation from John Stuart Mill comes from *The Subjection of Women* in John Stuart Mill and Harriet Taylor, *Essays on Sex Equality*, ed. A Rossi (University of Chicago Press, 1970), p. 148. The question whether there are essential differences between men's and women's nature is discussed in Deborah Rhode (ed.), *Theoretical Perspectives on Sexual Difference* (Yale University Press, 1990).

The feminist case against pornography is powerfully stated in Catherine MacKinnon, *Only Words* (Harper Collins, 1994).

For discussion about why and how women and cultural minorities should be included in democratic politics, see Anne Phillips, *The Politics of Presence* (Clarendon Press, 1995) and Iris Marion Young, *Inclusion and Democracy* (Oxford University Press, 2000).

On justice within the family, see especially Susan Moller Okin, *Justice, Gender and the Family* (Basic Books, 1989).

For those wanting to investigate the philosophical issues posed by affirmative action policies, a good place to start is Stephen Cahn, *The Affirmative Action Debate*, 2nd edn. (Routledge, 2002). See also Ronald Dworkin's essays collected in *A Matter of Principle* (Clarendon Press, 1986), part v.

Chapter 7

Benedict Anderson's influential idea of nations as imagined communities is developed in *Imagined Communities: Reflections on the Origins and Spread of Nationalism*, revised edn. (Verso, 1991). For contrasting interpretations of nationalism as a sociological phenomenon, see Ernest Gellner, *Nations and Nationalism* (Blackwell, 1983) and Anthony Smith, *National Identity* (Penguin, 1991).

My claim that national identity supports democracy and social justice is spelt out at greater length in *On Nationality* (Clarendon Press, 1995). For the argument that nationalism need not be detrimental to liberal values, see Yael Tamir, *Liberal Nationalism* (Princeton University Press, 1993).

Cosmopolitan political ideas are defended by David Held in *Democracy and the Global Order* (Polity, 1995). Cosmopolitan principles of justice are advocated in Charles Beitz, *Political Theory and International Relations* (new edn., Princeton University Press, 1999), Thomas Pogge, *Realizing Rawls* (Cornell University Press, 1989), and Charles Jones, *Global Justice: Defending Cosmopolitanism* (Oxford University Press, 1999).

Michael Walzer defends the view that 'thicker' principles of justice apply within national communities than across the world as a whole in *Thick and Thin: Moral Argument at Home and Abroad* (University of Notre Dame Press, 1994).

Immanuel Kant's essay 'Perpetual Peace' is included in *Kant's Political Writings*, ed. H. Reiss (Cambridge University Press, 1971). The quoted sentence in on p. 114.

For John Rawls's vision of a just world order as a 'realistic utopia' see *The Law of Peoples* (Harvard University Press, 1999).

Index

AMERICAN POLITICAL PARTIES AND ELECTIONS
A Very Short Introduction
Sandy L. Maisel

Few Americans and even fewer citizens of other nations understand the electoral process in the United States. Still fewer understand the role played by political parties in the electoral process or the ironies within the system. Participation in elections in the United States is much lower than in the vast majority of mature democracies. Perhaps this is because of the lack of competition in a country where only two parties have a true chance of winning, despite the fact that a large number of citizens claim allegiance to neither and think badly of both. Studying these factors, you begin to get a very clear picture indeed of the problems that underlay this much trumpeted electoral system.

www.oup.com/vsi

THE EUROPEAN UNION

A Very Short Introduction

John Pinder & Simon Usherwood

This *Very Short Introduction* explains the European Union in plain English. Fully updated for 2007 to include controversial and current topics such as the Euro currency, the EU's enlargement, and its role in ongoing world affairs, this accessible guide shows how and why the EU has developed from 1950 to the present. Covering a range of topics from the Union's early history and the ongoing interplay between 'eurosceptics' and federalists, to the single market, agriculture, and the environment, the authors examine the successes and failures of the EU, and explain the choices that lie ahead in the 21st century.

www.oup.com/vsi

GEOPOLITICS
A Very Short Introduction
Klaus Dodds

In certain places such as Iraq or Lebanon, moving a few feet either side of a territorial boundary can be a matter of life or death, dramatically highlighting the connections between place and politics. For a country's location and size as well as its sovereignty and resources all affect how the people that live there understand and interact with the wider world. Using wide-ranging examples, from historical maps to James Bond films and the rhetoric of political leaders like Churchill and George W. Bush, this Very Short Introduction shows why, for a full understanding of contemporary global politics, it is not just smart - it is essential - to be geopolitical.

'Engrossing study of a complex topic.'

Mick Herron, Geographical.

www.oup.com/vsi

GLOBALIZATION
A Very Short Introduction
Manfred Steger

'Globalization' has become one of the defining buzzwords of our time - a term that describes a variety of accelerating economic, political, cultural, ideological, and environmental processes that are rapidly altering our experience of the world. It is by its nature a dynamic topic - and this *Very Short Introduction* has been fully updated for 2009, to include developments in global politics, the impact of terrorism, and environmental issues. Presenting globalization in accessible language as a multifaceted process encompassing global, regional, and local aspects of social life, Manfred B. Steger looks at its causes and effects, examines whether it is a new phenomenon, and explores the question of whether, ultimately, globalization is a good or a bad thing.

www.oup.com/vsi

THE SOVIET UNION
A Very Short Introduction
Stephen Lovell

Almost twenty years after the Soviet Unions' end, what are we to make of its existence? Was it a heroic experiment, an unmitigated disaster, or a viable if flawed response to the modern world? Taking a fresh approach to the study of the Soviet Union, this Very Short Introduction blends political history with an investigation into the society and culture at the time. Stephen Lovell examines aspects of patriotism, political violence, poverty, and ideology; and provides answers to some of the big questions about the Soviet experience.

www.oup.com/vsi

THE UNITED NATIONS
A Very Short Introduction
Jussi M. Hanhimäki

With this much-needed introduction to the UN, Jussi Hanhimäki
engages the current debate over the organization's effectiveness
as he provides a clear understanding of how it was originally
conceived, how it has come to its present form, and how it
must confront new challenges in a rapidly changing world. After
a brief history of the United Nations and its predecessor, the
League of Nations, the author examines the UN's successes
and failures as a guardian of international peace and security,
as a promoter of human rights, as a protector of international law,
and as an engineer of socio-economic development.

www.oup.com/vsi

THE U.S CONGRESS
A Very Short Introduction
Donald Richie

The world's most powerful national legislature, the U. S. Congress, remains hazy as an institution. This *Very Short Introduction* to Congress highlights the rules, precedents, and practices of the Senate and House of Representatives, and offers glimpses into their committees and floor proceedings to reveal the complex processes by which they enact legislation. In *The U.S. Congress*, Donald A. Ritchie, a congressional historian for more than thirty years, takes readers on a fascinating, behind-the-scenes tour of Capitol Hill-pointing out the key players, explaining their behaviour, and translating parliamentary language into plain English.

www.oup.com/vsi

SOCIAL MEDIA
Very Short Introduction

Join our community

www.oup.com/vsi

- Join us online at the official Very Short Introductions **Facebook** page.
- Access the thoughts and musings of our authors with our online **blog**.
- Sign up for our monthly **e-newsletter** to receive information on all new titles publishing that month.
- Browse the full range of Very Short Introductions online.
- Read **extracts** from the Introductions for free.
- Visit our library of **Reading Guides**. These guides, written by our expert authors will help you to question again, why you think what you think.
- If you are a teacher or lecturer you can order inspection copies quickly and simply via our website.

ONLINE CATALOGUE
A Very Short Introduction

Our online catalogue is designed to make it easy to find your ideal Very Short Introduction. View the entire collection by subject area, watch author videos, read sample chapters, and download reading guides.

http://fds.oup.com/www.oup.co.uk/general/vsi/index.html